# Rigorism of Truth

*Series editor: Peter Uwe Hohendahl, Cornell University*

*Signale|TRANSFER* provides a unique channel for the transmission of critical German-language texts, newly translated into English, through to current debates on theory, philosophy, and social and cultural criticism. *Signale|TRANSFER* is a component of the series *Signale: Modern German Letters, Cultures, and Thought,* which publishes books in literary studies, cultural criticism, and intellectual history. *Signale* books are published under the joint imprint of Cornell University Press and Cornell University Library. Please see http://signale.cornell.edu/.

# Rigorism of Truth

## "Moses the Egyptian" and Other Writings on Freud and Arendt

Hans Blumenberg

Edited, with commentary and an afterword, by Ahlrich Meyer

Translated by Joe Paul Kroll

A Signale Book

Cornell University Press and Cornell University Library
Ithaca and London

Cornell University Press and Cornell University Library gratefully acknowledge the College of Arts & Sciences, Cornell University, for support of the Signale series.

Original German-language edition, *Der Rigorismus der Wahrheit: "Moses der Ägypter" und weitere Texte zu Freud und Arendt* von Hans Blumenberg; herausgegeben, kommentiert und mit einem Nachwort von Ahlrich Meyer

Copyright © Suhrkamp Verlag Berlin 2015

All rights reserved by and controlled through Suhrkamp Verlag Berlin.

All rights reserved. Except for brief quotations in a review, this book, or parts thereof, must not be reproduced in any form without permission in writing from the publisher. For information, address Cornell University Press, Sage House, 512 East State Street, Ithaca, New York 14850.

First published 2018 by Cornell University Press and Cornell University Library

Printed in the United States of America

Library of Congress Cataloging-in-Publication Data

Names: Blumenberg, Hans, author. | Meyer, Ahlrich, 1941– editor, writer of commentary, writer of afterword. | Kroll, Joe Paul, 1979– translator.
Title: Rigorism of truth : "Moses the Egyptian" and other writings on Freud and Arendt / Hans Blumenberg ; edited, with commentary and an afterword, by Ahlrich Meyer ; translated by Joe Paul Kroll.
Other titles: Rigorismus der Wahrheit. English
Description: Ithaca : Cornell University Press : Cornell University Library, 2017. | Series: Signale|transfer : German thought in translation | "A Signale book." | Includes bibliographical references.
Identifiers: LCCN 2017051823 (print) | LCCN 2017052395 (ebook) | ISBN 9781501714788 (pdf) | ISBN 9781501714696 (epub/mobi) | ISBN 9781501704819 | ISBN 9781501704819 (cloth ; alk. paper) | ISBN 9781501716720 (pbk. ; alk. paper)
Subjects: LCSH: Moses (Biblical leader) | Freud, Sigmund, 1856–1939. Mann Moses und die monotheistische Religion. | Arendt, Hannah, 1906–1975. Eichmann in Jerusalem.
Classification: LCC B3209.B833 (ebook) | LCC B3209.B833 R5413 2017 (print) | DDC 193—dc23
LC record available at https://lccn.loc.gov/2017051823

## Contents

| | |
|---|---|
| I. Moses the Egyptian | 1 |
| Editor's Notes | 12 |
| II. Excerpts and Preliminary Studies | 29 |
| On Sigmund Freud, *Moses and Monotheism* | 29 |
| On Hannah Arendt, *Eichmann in Jerusalem* | 41 |
| III. Thematically Related Texts from the Nachlass | 57 |
| Editor's Afterword | 71 |
| Editorial Note and Acknowledgments | 94 |
| Translator's Note | 96 |
| Illustration Credits | 98 |
| About the Authors | 99 |

# Rigorism of Truth

# I

# MOSES THE EGYPTIAN[1]

Moses, the Egyptian of pharaonic blood,[2] was invented by Sigmund Freud as a blow to his people, just as he had long before, in succession to the blows delivered by Copernicus and Darwin, delivered a blow to humanity with the unconscious.[3] He was one of those people who trust that the truth can achieve anything, even freedom, and thus from their love of truth[4] feel entitled to expect everything of themselves and of others. The year 1939 did not seem to him to be the absolutely wrong moment[5] to take from the beaten and humiliated [Jews] the man who, in the beginning, had founded their trust in history.[6] Freud had a low opinion of that history's documents;[7] to him, they were screen memories[8] devised to cover up the murderous outcome of a great deed, concealing the murder of Moses[9] in the desert and with it the failure of the most tremendous sublimation: the rising of the people from the mist of their libidinous state in Egypt to the lawfulness and purity of their forty-year education in the desert.[10] To Stefan Zweig,[11] Freud seems to have expressed qualms about depriving the Jews, in their most dreadful hour, when everything was being taken from them, of their best man. But what was that set against his making "a worthy exit," as he wrote to Hanns Sachs?[12] Ten years previously, he would have recognized in this trait the *vir impavidus*[13] as Horace[14] had exalted him, the stoic in the face of the end of the world, whom Freud had diagnosed as a case of narcissism.[15]

It was not even about the truth, as Freud himself knew very well. One would refuse to believe this if he had not himself shown so little confidence in his own discovery that he considered giving *Moses and Monotheism* the subtitle "a historical novel."[16] Perhaps "demi-novel" would have been the more apt term to convey how little it took to arouse mistrust in the founder of a national history, the heroic liberator, an alien representing the alien God—to use Marcion's phrase[17]—whom he alone claimed to have seen and heard.

Freud had the Egyptian prince Moses despise the people he wrested from slavery. He first read this contempt for "the mob," which could muster no faith in God's imagelessness, in the face of Michelangelo's Moses in Rome.[18] Egypt and the humiliations suffered at the pyramids were merely the consequence of the despicability of the patriarchal stories going all the way back to Joseph. Only a stranger could push all that aside, with a different God and a new law in sight, as though the covenants of that base prehistory had never existed, a prehistory that Moses may not have so much as heard recounted, having only ever dealt with this proletariat through an intermediary.[19] For all that is problematic about his discovery, there is one thing that Freud is quite correct in recognizing: only a stranger could exercise this measure of violence, this terrible weaning from gods and idols, from the comfortable anticipation of the next day, in order to compel renunciation in favor of the unknown. All of it came and could only come from the desert, from the overcoming of the temptation to keep the gods close at hand and as guarantors of the fleshpots.

But how could Moses do this for the benefit of those he despised? Here, Freud appears to have seen too little of what is political about his version of this story's beginning. It has always been the case that those who sought to win power for themselves and their idea have drawn on the potential of the despised, whom they could not love, but whom they promised themselves and others to love as soon as the despised became what they not yet were: worthy of power and beneficence. That is why an ideology of liberation must contain both: contempt for the present[20] as a result of the past *and* affection for the future as the result of the present. It is because Moses, the stranger, makes use of his adopted people only as the organ of his vision of things to come that he can chastise them so ruthlessly toward this end. The people must not remain what they are if he should be able not to despise them.

As soon as the liberated people became aware of being only the medium of an abstract revolt, they would murder him. They must do so as much as they must presently forget having done so, in order not to have to feel shame for the history thus gained. This would entail complicated rituals of guilt relief, and no historian would ever be able to decide whether it was worth the expense.

Nothing is less certain than that the truth wishes to be loved, can be loved, should be loved. Freud's "exposure" of the origins of Moses is also an "exposure" concerning himself and his relationship with the truth.[21] What he did in publishing *Moses and Monotheism*—which he would not have shown anyone in Vienna, so as not to endanger the existence of psychoanalysis[22]—so unhesitatingly in London,[23] although the self-confidence of his people was at stake, was to offer this people an analysis: not because the truth would set them free, but because Freud the scientist, who had always identified his patients with his own theoretical curiosity, had no qualms about transferring onto them that they must love and serve the truth.

In this situation, at the apex of Hitler's power and of the wretchedness of those he persecuted, there was no other motive to justify this publication but the absolutism of truth.[24] Freud did not believe that something like analysis could help the victims. Worse still, he did not even believe in the mechanism of repetition,[25] in which a stranger, one possessed by the frenzy of blood,[26] would once more renew the sublimating chastisements of the desert and yet, in the wildest autism, serve only the historical interest of the chastised.

None of these possibilities of his theory would justify Freud. He thought only of the "worthy exit" that he was preparing for himself.

Nonetheless, the Egyptian Moses, who drove the descendants of Jacob into the desert and whom they put to death, was also an incomparable model of that which was to follow only after Freud's last word.[27] That stranger had believed and desired to submit the people to his metaphysical idea of power; but in the long view of history, he had become the instrument of the people. Even the memories devised to cover up the murder of the cultural hero became the source of a ritualized self-punishment, whose forms and obligations, whose curtailments of life [*Lebensreduktionen*], were to anticipate the singular organization of the art of survival[28] that bestowed upon the Jews the ability to withstand all future deserts and captivities. The *felix culpa*[29] of Augustine in its worldliest form. The story's method[30] was embedded too deeply in memory for the story never to be able to assimilate even the most foreign object or person to itself.

Freud's great and last blow to humanity as embodied by its most afflicted turned out not to cause as much offense as he had expected[31] or of which he might have been ashamed. But it became an unexpected preliminary to something else, an aid to understanding the incredible. It turned out to be so only when, three decades later, another book caused offense, being unbearable to a new degree: Hannah Arendt's *Eichmann in Jerusalem*. The book, which emerged from a series of reports in the *New Yorker*,[32] first appeared in 1963, in German in 1964. It is subtitled *A Report on the Banality of Evil*. This phrase creates a line of continuity with Hannah Arendt's earlier work on the mechanism of the totalitarian state.[33] The dictatorship chose not the great demons and malefactors but the little family men[34] as accessories to its evil deeds, as functionaries of a malice of which they would never have been capable in the private and professional spheres of their bourgeois existence. As individuals, they had nothing of that which distinguished the successful actions they performed in massed anonymity: the dimension of the inconceivable. The many little men brought about the one big thing. Adolf Eichmann was something like the protagonist of such banality.

Hannah Arendt's rigorism[35] is very much like that of Sigmund Freud. She believes in the truth—that it is her truth, she can neither change nor prevent. Nobody has access to this relationship with what is truth to him, and nobody can be expected to have it. Hannah Arendt takes fearless analysis to be the therapy that she thinks she owes her comrades in affliction,[36] who have by now become the people of a state, although nothing is more alien to her than the dash of Freudianism that has now become customary. Even [the notion] that "resistance" should indicate the truth only symptomatically, indeed should be the first to release its salutary property, is something her project seems almost to assume. The outcry of indignation now strikes an *impavida*, the wreckage of the *orbis fractus* comes crashing upon her: another case of the kind that Freud, in 1930, used Horace's ode to diagnose as [one of] narcissism.[37] Which, after all, had meant even then: There is no love of truth. Maybe because there can be none.

In my turn prepared to court indignation, I am aghast at the deep-rooted similarities between *Moses and Monotheism* and *Eichmann in Jerusalem*. Similarities that can be discerned even in the equivalence of their effects. As Freud took Moses the man from his people, so Hannah Arendt took Adolf Eichmann from the State of Israel.

Some states are founded by their enemies.[38] Nobody else could have managed to circumvent the improbability of their existence. They exist, although or because everything that might otherwise have favored their establishment was too weak, too benign, too ideal, too literary, to prevail against a world of opposition. But then there they are, because nobody realistically wanted them except those who had nearly destroyed the conditions of their possibility. A state's founder can be the negative national hero. He must be killed, like Moses,[39] although he created the conditions of possibility of this nationhood.

Eichmann did not even do so against his own will. He studied his victims carefully and connected their utopia of nationhood with the idée fixe of self-purification.[40] In Zionism, he found what he had sought to create by force.[41] What is astonishing is that it is Zionism that Hannah Arendt could not forgive.[42] Why was this so? The organization of an idea corrupts what it strives to make real. It is preordained thus in the concept of the Idea ever since Plato devised it. What is more important still is that this pattern is now applied to the self-organization of the persecuted,[43] in which Hannah Arendt sees something like the suffocation of morality, the prevention of resistance, and thus once again a collaboration with the persecutors. Without the involvement of the Councils and Elders,[44] without the persecutors making arrangements with the institutional mode of existence, the entirety of extermination for which Eichmann was in the dock would not have functioned.

Does Hannah Arendt really believe this? It is the charge she brings against those who thought that something could be salvaged or who merely pretended to have come to a realistic appraisal of the situation. But it was a reality of the incredible, with which nobody can be expected to reckon.[45] What Hannah Arendt demands is to have thought the incredible, the possibility of resistance to a machine with which the world had for years failed to deal, and which for this undertaking mustered more ingenuity and imagination, accepting any detriment to already strained front lines, in order to bring at least this one project to completion,[46] if none of the others. The whole thing would not have taken place so discreetly if it had not worked so smoothly? Perhaps, but it would have worked. Hannah Arendt did not know all that the Nazis could do as long as it was accorded sufficient "priority."

Nonetheless, it is true that the self-organization of the persecuted deprived the individual of his chance to wager everything, to cry out loud just once. Every kind of organization reduces the possibility of making ultimate personal decisions, meeting absolute standards to which only the individual can ever be equal. Taking this thought to its final consequence means nothing less than that, to the political scientist, *the* very state, which is something like the continuation of the drive of the persecuted toward self-organization,[47] is suspect. Not because it is this state, but because it is *a* state at all, does it fail by the absolutism of those norms under which judgment might have been passed on Eichmann—if he could ever have been brought before this court.[48]

It is no mere coincidence and no *coincidentia oppositorum*[49] that the Nazis, when they were not sure of their autochthonous final solution,[50] had favored the idea of this state, had even imitated it in proto-autonomous forms within their occupied territories. Eichmann's entire knowledge of Judaism, as Hannah Arendt stresses, was derived from Theodor Herzl's *Judenstaat*,[51] and he would have taken the ideologue of this state quite exactly at his word, had not the outbreak of war stood in the way of such large-scale evictions. Extermination was, blasphemous though it may sound, only a variant forced by circumstance[52] of the idea of relocation to "firm ground under the feet of the Jews."[53] And then there is a scene that, in retrospect, seems unimaginable, the farce [*das Schelmenstück*] of Eichmann's invitation to Palestine by Jewish emissaries.[54] These analogies, verging on the inconceivable yet politically almost inevitable, determine the odium that the political scientist finds across the full extent of the Eichmann case. To study such incomprehension in its conditions is, viewed another quarter century later,[55] a singular specimen for a theory of nonconceptuality.[56]

On the face of it, to observe the observer is only to perform an experiment in eminent acuity. Arendt sees everything juridically,[57] for she does not want to admit a state of exception and, as a citizen of the United States, has no need to do so. A historic scene was not reenacted,[58] but performed belatedly: a legitimacy emerging from, and only from, the state of exception.[59] The only death sentence ever passed in Israel, in spite of the danger it has faced from within and without. The Federal Republic of Germany, though arising from sheer nothingness, would have been unable to punish even the destroyer of the Reich as whose legal successor it emerged. Then what of Eichmann?

Of course it was the prosecution in the trial, bound by instructions, upon which the critic of the court pours her scorn, finding it incompetent to prove what it had announced it would prove[60]— although, had the prosecution succeeded in doing so, the indictment would have fallen outside the scope of the one special law.[61] The worst thing was that, even after the execution, the prosecution made public psychiatric reports that qualified Eichmann as sadistic and murderous, at any rate a pathological figure, whose legal responsibility would then have had to be ascertained.[62] But even in the absence of this clinical aspect, Hannah Arendt had long made up her mind that an intelligence of such a low order would never have come up with the final solution himself. Eichmann thus stands for the thesis stated much earlier, in her theory of totalitarianism, according to which the ever-eager functionary came from the background of the petit bourgeois run wild and the manipulable paterfamilias[63] or became involved, as did this particular specimen, because he was "bored to distraction."[64]

Finally, the witnesses.[65] They projected onto the accused everything that had been done to them. They thus saw him even where he had not been, but might as well have, while he was elsewhere, doing much the same. Perhaps the witnesses did not believe in the court in the Valley of Jehoshaphat near Jerusalem,[66] where judgment would be passed not only on what someone had done, but also on what he would have done. The court was right to apply judicial norms in leaving such things aside and not to consider them in their sentencing. From a legal perspective, there is no such thing as a singular case, nor can there be, for jurisdiction depends on subsumption. But there can be no subsumption where the organizer of a genocide is, in a kind of state ceremony, made a scapegoat,[67] in part and even not least for that which he would only potentially have done. One may be fervently opposed to this ritual; but first one must have understood what it means to the others [i.e., the victims and witnesses], and to what insignificance this meaning condemns one's criticism.

Hannah Arendt's point is that this scapegoat stands for *those* sins that the others committed or might have committed, that is, the Germans.[68] And this event certainly attracts attempts at delegation, hopes for the expunction of guilt, and datings for the finality of closing the file.[69] With all respect for the rightness of such considerations, one must say that universal moralism fails to touch what is necessary only in a mythical sense.[70] It was, after all, the same state that accepted reparations,[71] which could never possibly be a moral compensation, but an act of reason of state: every day's delay, that much became clear anyhow, could only devalue politically what was anyhow impossible to evaluate morally.

What the mythical act must concentrate in *one* figure, because it cannot otherwise attain the level of intuitiveness[72] that every claim to legitimacy requires, appears diffuse to the political scientist. Contrary to her self-definition, Arendt's thinking in this matter is neither philosophical nor politological, but sociological: society may be culpable, but then it no longer allows for principal culprits.[73] That is why *Eichmann in Jerusalem* is above all a book against Eichmann's sole guilt.[74] This sole guilt, however, is the political core of the process, which would have been disturbed or even destroyed by any question as to who had made the murderous bureaucrats possible and might now be hiding behind the imaginary vastness of the negative hero. But one cannot have both at once: the analysis and the myth.[75]

Hannah Arendt, who preferred to be addressed as a political scientist and was embarrassed when suspected of philosophy,[76] was a moralist. Her book is a document of rigorism, the definition of which is the refusal to acknowledge an ultimate and inexorable dilemma in human action. One can and must at all times be certain of what is to be done and what remains the right thing to do. To moralize the political[77] implies that it too can be fraught with dilemmas only on the surface, but must in the final instance be capable of the unity of the will.

For this reason, it is necessary to confront the political scientist with her own dilemma:[78] the very clown to whom she sees Eichmann degraded before all eyes seems to her underexposed on the stage of this *national* tribunal. She would like to see his figure from the vantage point of humanity, out of a reluctance to leave it to Zionism. Her *Pathosformel*[79] is magnificent, but misses everything that distinguishes this process: because Eichmann had appointed himself judge over who was and who was not permitted to inhabit the earth, nobody, following Arendt, could henceforth be expected to share the earth with the maker of such a claim.[80] For Arendt, he therefore belonged before a tribunal of all human beings.[81] But that is precisely what would have removed him from his function of entering the national myth as the vanquished necessary enemy, who may have claimed victims but, in doing so, had foisted on their sacrifice the only meaning still possible. Yet Hannah Arendt considered it a greater task still to expose the victims of an atrocity as its accessories,[82] because that would be the kind of moral situation that might recur at any time.

It is the line of thought in which moral rigorism and apolitical sociologism converge:[83] the criminal could only be the way he was because his victims were the way they were. A tribunal of all humanity, a secularized form of the Last Judgment,[84] would have to pass sentence on the victims, too. As a crime against humanity, however, the case of Eichmann would have been "internationalized," not a crime of the most monstrous singularity against the Jewish people and not the warrant, impervious to any realistic objection, for [the foundation of] this state. For that reason, there was also to be no internalization of the accused's guilt toward a personal sense of wrongdoing; and it is no coincidence that Eichmann evidently lacked any such thing.[85] The monster's conscience is clear. It is put to death, not punished, made to disappear from the face of the earth. Even the ashes are scattered not over the Holy Land, but over the sea.[86] Here, Hannah Arendt sees the syndrome of "long-forgotten propositions"[87] according to which everything had supposedly taken place, including those of *ius talionis*[88] and even outright revenge.

When, in 1964, Günter Gaus confronts her with some passages from *Eichmann in Jerusalem* on television,[89] she keeps thinking that what she stands accused of was a lack of piety toward the victims.[90] She does not perceive the hiatus between the categories.[91] In failing to recognize the public and political status of the trial as staking a claim to national legitimacy, she sees the victims and their descendants as engaging in an act of retribution. Even if this act of state should not have been a particularly fine example of the fulfillment of its intentions, it is all the more important to see what was or must have been the intention. It was precisely not the business of the victims' descendants to avenge them, but the business of a state's people to have captured and sentenced its historic enemy and negative founder of the state, just as the Germans must have wished[92] to have tried the negative founder of their rump states, although they would have had no law under which to do so but that of unique historic right. This statement is not meant to deny that those who were not just victims, not even only partly responsible victims, would certainly not have managed to do so. But they too would hardly have tolerated seeing the destroyer of their state, indeed, the denier of their right to exist,[93] as a figure of ridicule rather than as the demon it took a world of others to overcome.

To undemonize Hitler[94] was something historians could dare only at a delay and only because the Germans had not been capable of bringing him to justice. Eichmann, who was judged in the heart of the state that would not have arisen without him, could stand before this court only as the phenotype of nondescriptness.[95] He became the self-desubstantiating phantom[96] of a figure that was able to "make" history only once he had been captured and killed. This is why it was never to be said that this man had been a clown (thus A. Reif, *Gespräche mit Hannah Arendt*, 26).[97] To have captured and executed a pathetic straw man discredits the act of state that was and had to be made of it.

Hannah Arendt could not have written this book any differently from the way she wrote it; every reader will be persuaded of this. That is precisely why she ought not to have written it.[98] Would it have been impossible, then, to write a book of this rank on this singular event at all? Though it is an anachronism, the thought may be framed in the irrealis mood: Sigmund Freud could have written this book. This may sound like a mere witty paradox after all that it was necessary to say on the ruthlessness of *Moses and Monotheism*. But that was a question less of Freud's vision of the stranger who had come to save and purify a people than of the time of the book's publication. What Freud, if he can be imagined witnessing it, would have immediately recognized is the mythical dimension of killing the negative hero of the state. Here it was not the father of the primal horde,[99] who had pursued his sons with his cannibalism and whom they had to kill in order to survive, but the founder of the state, who had become so by means of the greatest massacre in history[100]—and by history's devious ways. On this occasion, too, Freud would not have written a book apt to please his people. The stranger in Eichmann required no revealing. He was just that. Freud would, one hardly dares to think it, have projected onto Moses the Egyptian, who was barred from setting foot in the

Promised Land, the monstrosity of Adolf Eichmann, whose ashes were more than that very country could bear.

## Editor's Notes

1. The following text was translated directly from Blumenberg's typescript in the Deutsches Literaturarchiv (DLA) Marbach, and checked against Ahlrich Meyer's transcription. All emphasis is Blumenberg's own. Blumenberg's practice in the text was to use 'single' quotation marks throughout, with "double" quotation marks reserved for book titles. Underlining was used for emphasis as well as to indicate quotations from the work under discussion. I have modified these principles to give the text a smoother appearance. Elsewhere in the volume, I have followed Meyer's transcriptions. (Trans.)

2. Since 1933/34, Freud pursued the idea that Moses had in fact been an Egyptian, who had transmitted to the Jewish people the monotheistic cult of Akhenaten. His speculations were based on the research of Egyptologists and historians, notably Eduard Meyer, James H. Breasted, and Ernst Sellin.

3. Freud repeatedly compared himself to Copernicus and Darwin. Beside the "two major blows [*Kränkungen*]" dealt by science to the "naïve self-love of men," a cosmological and a biological one, he placed his discovery as the "third and most wounding blow." Sigmund Freud, *Introductory Lectures on Psycho-Analysis*, in *SE*, 16:284–85.

4. Many sources attest to Freud's claim to truth. At a gathering of his students in 1930, for instance, he declared: "My single motive was the love of truth." Richard F. Sterba, *Reminiscences of a Viennese Psychoanalyst* (Detroit: Wayne State University Press, 1982), 115. After completing the third part of the Moses book, Freud wrote to the scientist Charles Singer on 31 October 1938: "Needless to say, I don't like offending my own people, either. But what can I do about it? I have spent my whole life standing up for what I have considered to be the scientific truth, even when it was uncomfortable and unpleasant for my fellow men." *Letters of Sigmund Freud*, selected and edited by Ernst L. Freud (New York: Basic Books, 1960), 453. See also below, p. 13, n. 11.

5. After the pogroms of 1938, the number of Jews expelled from Germany and Austria rose sharply, with forced emigration reaching its peak in 1939. Freud emigrated from Vienna to London in early June 1938, following the *Anschluss* of Austria to the German Reich. In London, he completed work on *Moses and Monotheism*, which he had begun in 1934, and which was published in German by Albert de Lange of Amsterdam in March 1939.

6. In his introduction to the first part of *Moses and Monotheism*, which appeared already in 1937 in the journal *Imago* (vol. 23, no. 1, pp. 5–13) under the title "Moses ein Ägypter," Freud wrote: "To deprive a people of the man they take pride in as the greatest of their own is not a thing to be gladly or carelessly undertaken, least of all by someone who is himself one of them." These lines reappeared in the book (*SE*, 23:7).

Following the book's publication, Freud's biographer Ernest Jones reports that speculation was rife as to the motives Freud might have had in writing the book: "One malicious [supposition] was that he was venting his secret hatred of the Jews by depriving them of their cherished leader [. . .]." Ernest Jones, *The Life and Work of Sigmund Freud*, vol. 3, *The Last Phase, 1919–1939* (London: The Hogarth Press, 1957), 395.

7. On 3 March 1936, Freud told Ernest Jones that his work was to contain "a refutation of the Jewish national mythology." Jones, *Life and Work*, 3:222; see *SE*, 23:43–44.

8. Freud used the term "screen memories" to describe the associative displacement of significant impressions from early childhood, whose reproduction in adulthood is resisted, by indifferent childhood memories. See, e.g., Freud, *The Psychopathology of Everyday Life*, in *SE*, 6:43–52.

9. Based on research by the Old Testament scholar and archaeologist Edgar Sellin, Freud assumed "that the Egyptian Moses was murdered by the Jews and the religion he had introduced abandoned" (*SE*, 23:37). This assumption tallied with the theory of parricide Freud had first developed in 1913 in *Totem and Taboo* (*SE*, 13:140–146).

10. Exodus 16.

11. Stefan Zweig visited Freud in London in June 1938; no record of Freud having mentioned any reservations to him can be found. (Blumenberg was possibly thinking of comments made by Freud to Arnold Zweig here.) In fact, Stefan Zweig rather admired Freud's "frankness" (*Freimut*) and encouraged him not to let himself be swayed by a "foolish Jewish nationalism," one "which feels robbed because you represent the Jewish religion in part as one that is alien and adopted." Stefan Zweig, *Briefwechsel*, ed. Jeffrey B. Berlin et al. (Frankfurt: Fischer, 1987), 214–215. However, Freud, who had from an early stage been prepared for negative reactions from Jewish circles (cf. *Letters of Sigmund Freud*, 440, 453–454) received several warnings in 1938 against publishing the Moses book. To Arnold Zweig, for instance, he wrote on 28 June 1938 of a letter he had received from a Jewish American who had implored him "not to deprive our poor unhappy people of the one consolation remaining to them in their misery." *The Letters of Sigmund Freud and Arnold Zweig*, ed. Ernst L. Freud (London: The Hogarth Press, 1970), 163. At a meeting with representatives of YIVO (Yiddisher Vissenshaftlikher Institut/Institute for Jewish Research) in London in November 1938, Freud spoke of "warnings he had received from Jewish sources" not to publish his "views on Moses and Monotheism": "But to him the truth was sacred and he could not renounce his rights as a scientist to voice it." Jones, *Life and Work*, 3:253.

12. The psychoanalyst Hanns Sachs belonged to the circle of Freud's pupils and was for a time the editor of the journal *Imago*; in his memoirs he quotes from a letter to him from Freud dated 12 March 1939: "The *Moses*, printed in German at Albert de Lange, made its appearance here today in two copies. Quite a worthy exit, I believe." Hanns Sachs, *Freud: Master and Friend* (Cambridge, MA: Harvard University Press, 1944), 184. The letter is also mentioned in Ernest Jones's biography of Freud, where the passage in question sounds less harsh: "The Moses is not an unworthy leavetaking." Jones, *Life and Work*, 3:259.

13. "The man of firm and righteous will" (Horace, *Odes* 3.3, trans. John Conington).

14. Horace, *Odes* 3.3: "Si fractus illabatur orbis / Impavidum ferient ruinae" (Should Nature's pillar'd frame give way, / That wreck would strike one fearless head; trans. John Conington). Freud was familiar with this ode, which he quoted several times (cf. *Letters of Sigmund Freud*, 438, and the following note). Blumenberg, too, liked to refer to these verses, and once accused the theologian Rudolf Bultmann of having misquoted them. See Blumenberg's review of Bultmann's *History and Eschatology*, Gnomon 31, no. 2 (1959): 163–166, esp. 166; cf. Hans Blumenberg, *Höhlenausgänge* (Frankfurt: Suhrkamp, 1989), 281; Blumenberg, *Die Vollzähligkeit der Sterne* (Frankfurt: Suhrkamp, 1997), 267–268; Blumenberg, *Zu den Sachen und zurück*, ed. Manfred Sommer (Frankfurt: Suhrkamp, 2002), 29. It may be of interest that Husserl, persecuted by the Nazis in 1933, also recalled this ode. See Markus Asper and Sebastian Luft, "Consolatio philologiae: Horaz, c. III, 1–8 bei Edmund Husserl," *Philologus* 144, no. 1 (2000): 361–374.

15. On 20 March 1930, Freud's treatise *Civilization and Its Discontents* was discussed at a meeting of the Vienna Mittwochsgesellschaft (Wednesday Club). On this occasion, Freud quoted the two lines from Horace and translated them himself: "If the firmament should break to pieces over him, / the fragments will bury a fearless man" (Sterba, *Reminiscences*, 114). But he altered the meaning of these verses, as Blumenberg recorded on an undated index card under the heading "Horace's *Impavidus* Is Narcissism Typified": "The fearless one imagined by Horace is the stoic by inner moral strength, whereas Freud reads him as the narcissistic type" (see below, p. 35). He elaborated on this elsewhere: "Sigmund Freud was the first to see that the unflappable type was not the realistic one, i.e., of an active confrontation with that whose aspect he is able to bear. The stoic, whose praises Horace sings as the figure unafraid amid the world's collapse, appears to Freud as the narcissistic type. Perhaps Freud's treatise on 'Civilization and Its Discontents' of 1930 is, compared to Spengler's 'Decline,' the more radical eschatology, written as it was on the brink of a more severe catastrophe than defeat in the First World War. Its greater radicalism consists of the smaller admixture of consolation." Typescript ESC [Eschatology] X, fol. 15b, DLA Marbach, Nachlass Hans Blumenberg.

16. In a letter to Arnold Zweig, Freud explained the point of departure of his work on the Moses book and referred to the planned title: "The Man Moses, a Historical Novel" (*Letters of Sigmund Freud and Arnold Zweig*, 91).

17. Marcion (ca. 85–160) was the founder of a dualistic theology that distinguished the malign creator god of the Old Testament from the merciful god of the New Testament, calling the latter the "alien God." Blumenberg inverts the meaning by adopting Freud's presuppositions: the "alien God" is the one introduced to the Jews by Moses. Blumenberg discussed Marcion in some detail in the context of his own studies on Gnosticism, e.g., in *The Legitimacy of the Modern Age*, trans. Robert M. Wallace (Cambridge, MA: MIT Press, 1983), 129–130; and *Work on Myth*, trans. Robert M. Wallace (Cambridge, MA: MIT Press, 1985), 181–199.

18. Freud repeatedly visited the Roman church of San Pietro in Vincoli to see Michelangelo's statue of Moses. He had, he wrote in 1914, always "essayed to support the angry scorn of the hero's glance! Sometimes I have crept cautiously out of the half-gloom of the interior as though I myself belonged to the mob upon whom his eye is turned—the mob which can hold fast no conviction, which has neither faith nor patience, and which rejoices when it has regained its illusory idols." Freud, *The Moses of Michelangelo*, in *SE*, 13:213.

19. Aaron, Moses's brother.
20. A frequently reiterated critical notion of Blumenberg's, marked by a distrust of any idea of progress and ideology of liberation that denigrates the present in favor of the future, demands sacrifices for an uncertain goal, and places the burden of history on entire generations. Cf. Hans Blumenberg, "Ernst Cassirers gedenkend," in *Wirklichkeiten, in denen wir leben* (Stuttgart: Reclam, 1981), 163–172, esp. 168–169; Blumenberg, *Lebenszeit und Weltzeit* (Frankfurt: Suhrkamp, 1986), 114, 225; Blumenberg, *Care Crosses the River*, trans. Paul Fleming (Stanford, CA: Stanford University Press, 2010), 149–152; Blumenberg, *Höhlenausgänge*, 751.
21. See above, p. 12, n. 4.
22. Beginning in 1934 Freud, in his correspondence with Arnold Zweig, expressed reservations about publishing his research on *Moses and Monotheism*, fearing, among other things, a ban on psychoanalysis in Vienna, given that the Catholic priest Wilhelm Schmidt (who was also an ethnologist and an opponent of Freud's) determined the country's policy. However, Freud gave further reasons for his caution before publishing the first two treatises in the journal *Imago* in 1937. One such reason was his "opinion about the weakness of [his] historical construction." *Letters of Sigmund Freud and Arnold Zweig*, 92, 97, 98, 104; cf. *SE*, 23:75–58, 103–104.
23. Blumenberg made several excerpts and notes concerning the genesis of *Moses and Monotheism*. In his London exile, Freud revised the third treatise on "The Man Moses," which had, according to Freud, already been written in Vienna, but was yet unpublished. It appeared in book form in 1939 alongside the two parts published in 1937. At this point in time, Freud no longer gave any heed to reservations against publication.
24. "Absolutism of truth" is one of several critical terms used by Blumenberg to characterize human self-assertion: *The Legitimacy of the Modern Age* (1966) describes the early modern turn against the "theological absolutism" of the late Middle Ages. In *Work on Myth* (1979), Blumenberg refers to the "absolutism of reality" as the epitome of "not having control over the conditions of our existence." Absolutism of truth is equivalent to the rigorism of the claim to truth. Blumenberg nowhere questioned the transfer of the term "absolutism" from theology and political science to philosophy. Odo Marquard believed that he had identified the foundational thought of Blumenberg's philosophy in the "idea of the relief [*Entlastung*] from the absolute." Odo Marquard, "Entlastung vom Absoluten," in *Die Kunst des Überlebens: Nachdenken über Hans Blumenberg*, ed. Franz Josef Wetz and Hermann Timm (Frankfurt: Suhrkamp, 1999), 17–27, 20.
25. An allusion to Freud's theory of the compulsion to repeat, first presented in *Beyond the Pleasure Principle* (1920; *SE*, 18:1–64). Blumenberg also saw repetition as a fundamental trait of myth; see his landmark essay "Wirklichkeitsbegriff und Wirkungspotential des Mythos," in *Terror und Spiel: Probleme der Mythenrezeption*, ed. Manfred Fuhrmann (Munich: Fink, 1971), 11–66, 24.
26. The stranger "possessed by the frenzy of blood" is Hitler—the text permits no other reading, though the parallel with Freud's Moses figure is hard to stomach. The idea that Hitler, "in the wildest autism," i.e., in his murderous racism, should ultimately have served the "historical interest" of the Jews, seems equally scandalous. This idea was later to recur with reference to Adolf Eichmann.

27. I.e., Freud's use of the term "a worthy exit" in the March 1939 letter to Hanns Sachs. The Second World War began soon after, providing Hitler with the conditions in which the "final solution of the Jewish question," i.e., the physical elimination of European Jewry, could be carried out.

28. Blumenberg's papers contain various excerpts and notes that testify to his interest in the "art of survival" [*Überlebenskunst*] and the resilience that the Jews drew from the Mosaic tradition over the course of millennia. An early instance is a 1954 essay on the Spanish Jewish philosopher Maimonides (1135–1204): "The Mosaic law, a relic ripped from its context in the life-ways of millennia, thus became the formative power behind the formal constancy and hardness of surviving Jewry" ("Moses Maimonides und der Anteil des spanischen Judentums am europäischen Mittelalter," typescript, fol. 4, DLA Marbach, Nachlass Hans Blumenberg; there is no evidence of the essay having been published). Similar remarks may be quoted from Freud's *Moses*, e.g., his mention of the "unexampled capacity for resistance" and sense of self of the Jewish people, who for millennia had defied "misfortunes and ill treatment" and "developed special character-traits" imprinted upon them by Moses (*SE*, 23:105).

29. The Exultet of the Roman Catholic Easter vigil mass contains the line "O felix culpa, quae talem ac tantum meruit habere redemptorem!" (O happy fault that earned for us so great, so glorious a redeemer!) This goes back to Saint Augustine and implies an answer to the problem of theodicy: "Melius enim iudicavit de malis benefacere, quam mala nulla esse permittere" (For God judged it better to bring good out of evil than not to permit any evil to exist). Augustine, *Enchiridion*, 27, trans. A. C. Outler, http://www.tertullian.org/fathers/augustine_enchiridion_02_trans.htm. Hannah Arendt rejected this concept of evil; see the afterword for this.

30. *Das Verfahren der Geschichte*, which can also mean "the historical method or process." (Trans.)

31. Perhaps on account of its date of publication, Freud's *Moses* stirred no controversy among the Jewish or the non-Jewish public comparable to that surrounding Arendt's courtroom report.

32. The magazine commissioned Hannah Arendt to report as its courtroom correspondent from the Eichmann trial in Jerusalem. Eichmann spent April to June 1961 in Israel. Arendt's series of five articles, entitled "A Reporter at Large: Eichmann in Jerusalem," appeared in February and March 1963. The book edition, published soon afterward, in May 1963, was slightly revised and expanded by Arendt.

33. Blumenberg is referring to Arendt's essay "Organized Guilt and Universal Responsibility," which was written in the United States in 1944 and published first in English, as "German Guilt" in *Jewish Frontier* 12 (1945), and then in German in the first issue of the monthly *Die Wandlung* (1946) and subsequently in Hannah Arendt, *Sechs Essays* (Heidelberg: Lambert Schneider, 1948), 33–47. Blumenberg does not appear to have read Arendt's major work, *The Origins of Totalitarianism* (1951; first German edition, 1955).

34. This is taken from the aforementioned essay "Organized Guilt," in which Arendt examined the transformation of "good family men" into functionaries of Himmler's murder organization; see Blumenberg's excerpt below, p. 42. That

Arendt should have described "in her analysis 'The Origins of Totalitarianism' [. . .] the figure of the paterfamilias in the machinery of murder," as Blumenberg repeatedly notes (see, e.g., "Familienväter," typescript, DLA Marbach, Nachlass Hans Blumenberg), hardly does that work justice.

35. The charge of "rigorism" forms the link between the two heterogeneous parts of this text. There are many sources for Arendt's claim to truth. In the television interview with Günter Gaus, to which Blumenberg refers in the following, she answered the repeated question if it was permissible to "be silent about the truth" by stating that what was at stake was "really a matter of truths of fact" rather than "a matter of opinions," before posing the counter-question "Why shouldn't one speak the truth?" Hannah Arendt, "'What Remains? The Language Remains': A Conversation with Günter Gaus" (broadcast on the German television network ZDF, 28 October 1964), in *The Portable Hannah Arendt*, ed. Peter Baehr (New York: Penguin, 2000), 3–22, on 18. In her 1968 essay "Truth and Politics," she wrote that the controversy over the Eichmann book and the lies spread about its contents and even about facts it reported had given her cause to consider "whether it is always legitimate to tell the truth" (in *Portable Hannah Arendt*, 545–575, on 545).

36. There is no reason to suppose that Arendt meant to say that she owed the Jews or the State of Israel a "therapy." The claim rests on the analogy with Freud and psychoanalysis.

37. *Impavida, orbis fractus*: see above, pp. 13–14, nn. 13 and 14.

38. This is true of Israel as it is of no other state, for there can be no doubt that the establishment of a Jewish state was possible only as a historical consequence of the Holocaust. This makes it all the more puzzling that Blumenberg drew this entire paragraph from an earlier note referring not to Israel, but to Finland (see below, p. 45).

39. That Eichmann had to be killed "like Moses" is an analogy drawn from a link between the matter at stake in the Jerusalem trial and Freud's postulation of a parricide perpetrated against the Egyptian Moses.

40. This refers to the Nazi ideology of purifying the "people as a body" (*Volkskörper*), in this instance the expulsion of the Jews from Germany.

41. From 1935 to 1938, Eichmann worked in Department II 112 ("Jewry") of the Main Office of the Security Police (*Sicherheitspolizei*, SD), where he was in charge of the portfolio "Zionists"; he monitored the activities of Zionist organizations and became an expert on "Jewish emigration."

42. Already before fleeing Germany in 1933, Hannah Arendt had turned to Zionism under the influence of Kurt Blumenfeld, the president of the German Federation of Zionists; during her exile in Paris she worked for Youth Aliyah, which organized the emigration of Jewish youngsters to Palestine. After emigrating to the United States herself in 1941, she called for an active involvement of Jews in the European resistance to Hitler, while becoming increasingly critical of Zionist demands for the establishment of a Jewish state comprising all of Palestine. She broke with Zionism in 1944. See Hannah Arendt, "Zionism Reconsidered" (1944), in *Jewish Writings* (New York: Schocken, 2007), 342–374.

43. The term blurs the distinction between the manifold forms in which Jewish life in Europe organized itself and the compulsory Jewish organizations that the

Nazis set up everywhere during the Second World War, like the Jewish Councils (*Judenräte*) and Councils of Elders, into which recognized representatives of local Jewish communities were often co-opted.

44. Blumenberg is referring to Arendt's charges against "Jewish leaders" and "Jewish Councils" of cooperation with the Nazis in the destruction of their own people (she used the term "collaboration" only in her private correspondence). In the first American edition of *Eichmann in Jerusalem*, Arendt wrote: "Wherever Jews lived, there were recognized Jewish leaders, and this leadership, almost without exception, cooperated in one way or another, for one reason or another, with the Nazis. The whole truth was that if the Jewish people had really been unorganized and leaderless, there would have been chaos and plenty of misery but the total number of victims would hardly have been between four and a half and six million people" (*EJ*, 125). In the revised edition and the German translation, she supports this calculation with information on the Amsterdam Joodsche Rad and figures for rescued and deported Jews, supplied by the Dutch historian Louis de Jong. They do not, however, permit the conclusion Arendt drew that half the victims of the Holocaust "could have saved themselves if they had not followed the instructions of the Jewish Councils" (*EJ*, 125; cf. *EJG*, 162).

45. Blumenberg's objection is of crucial significance to the historical assessment of the role of the *Judenräte*. Many testimonies indicate that at the time the persecuted and those engaged in negotiations with the Nazis did not know or at any rate did not believe that the deported Jews were to be murdered. See Insa Meinen, *Die Shoah in Belgien* (Darmstadt: Wissenschaftliche Buchgesellschaft, 2009), 73–75, for an exemplary study. Blumenberg, who was arrested in early 1945 and, alongside hundreds of other "Jewish half-castes," taken to one of the Organisation Todt's forced-labor camps, is probably speaking of his own experience here. A posthumously published text discussed the situation of the *Halbjuden* in the Third Reich in the following terms: "It was known who had been endangered how and by what decree or which use of discretionary power. So someone had a Jewish father? Well, they didn't murder [such people] right away [. . .]. But, the point is, nobody knew how far it would go. The one preserved copy of the minutes of the 'Wannsee Conference' of January 1942 still gives [one] an idea of where things were headed and what [*sic*] could be executed any day without so much as the flick of a pen." Hans Blumenberg, "Ob man sagen darf: 'Ich habe Angst,'" in *Ein mögliches Selbstverständnis* (Stuttgart: Reclam, 1997), 21–26, 23.

46. Beginning at the latest in 1942, the Nazi regime is known to have accorded the enactment of the "final solution" highest priority.

47. From its foundation, the State of Israel has regarded itself as part of the Zionist tradition, but not as the continuation of Jewish "self-organization" during the Nazi era.

48. Karl Jaspers had suggested that Eichmann be sentenced not by an Israeli court, but by an international tribunal (Jaspers in a radio interview with François Bondy, reprinted in *Der Monat* 152 [1961]: 15–19; see also Jaspers's letter to Arendt of 14 February 1961, in Hannah Arendt and Karl Jaspers, *Correspondence, 1926–1969*, ed. Lotte Kohler and Hans Sahner [New York: Harcourt Brace, 1992], 224–226). Arendt adopted this position (*EJ*, 252). Before and during the Eichmann trial, objections were raised from various quarters, including Eichmann's defense

counsel Servatius, against the trial, and the jurisdiction of the Jerusalem court was called into question.

49. The coincidence (i.e., concurrence) of opposites, a term coined by Nicholas of Cues (Nicolaus Cusanus, 1401–1461), which Blumenberg called a *Sprengmetapher*. The latter term occurs in several places in Blumenberg's work and has been translated variously as "metaphor of explosion" (*Legitimacy of the Modern Age*, 490–492), "explosive metaphorics" (Hans Blumenberg, *Paradigms for a Metaphorology*, trans. with an afterword by Robert Savage [Ithaca, NY: Cornell University Press and Cornell University Library, 2011], 125), and "explosive metaphor" (Hans Blumenberg, *Shipwreck with Spectator: Paradigm of a Metaphor for Existence*, trans. Stephen Rendall [Cambridge, MA: MIT Press, 1997], 90). See also Blumenberg's selection from the works of Cusanus: Hans Blumenberg, ed., *Die Kunst der Vermutung* (Bremen: Schünemann, 1957), 72.

50. Nazi plans for the "final solution of the Jewish question" became more radical between 1940 and 1942. Only when various territorial "solutions" (Madagascar Plan, resettlement in "Jewish reservations," or deportations to the occupied Soviet Union) had proved impracticable was the physical elimination of European Jews decided upon. Blumenberg's knowledge of this historical process, the study of which has advanced since the 1990s, was clearly only rudimentary, or else he could not have thought that, with their resettlement plans, the Nazis had promoted the idea of a Jewish state or imitated its preliminary stages. The same can be said with regard to Jewish self-government within the ghettos of Europe or in Theresienstadt.

51. Herzl's book *Der Judenstaat* (*The Jewish State*) was published in 1896. Reporting from the trial, Arendt wrote that it had been "the first serious book that [Eichmann] ever read and it made a lasting impression on him," converting him "promptly and forever to Zionism" (*EJ*, 40). It is doubtful that Eichmann really read Herzl's book. In the so-called Sassen Interviews, recorded in Argentina in 1957, as well as during the trial, he confused it with Adolf Böhm's *Die Zionistische Bewegung*, 2nd ed. (Berlin: Jüdischer Verlag, 1935–37). With reference to his time working at the SD main office, he put the following on record: "[. . .] we want a 'final solution,' that was the word that, following Herzl, Theodor Herzl, dished up by Adolf Böhm, was so to speak suggested to me in his '*Judenstaat*,' for after all I devoured this '*Judenstaat*.'" Quoted in Irmtrud Wojak, *Eichmanns Memoiren* (Frankfurt: Campus, 2001), 89.

52. The Madagascar Plan, which had been briefly pursued in spring 1940 and which entailed the "resettlement" of Jews in an overseas colony, was abandoned when the course of the war made it impracticable. Yet that the murder of the Jews should have been "only a variant forced by circumstance" of earlier, territorial plans for a "final solution" is a simplification that overlooks the complex processes of making and enacting the decisions leading to genocide. An index card from 1978, a preliminary to this passage, shows that Blumenberg originally based his claims on Eichmann's testimony, as recorded by Hannah Arendt. In the older version, when Eichmann "was no longer able to evacuate [the Jews] (because of the war), extermination was to him [!] a remolding of the idea of expulsion." Cf. *EJ*, 77.

53. This is a quotation from Hannah Arendt's account (*EJ*, 41, 56, 76, 99) and can be traced to Eichmann's own statements. At the 75th session of the trial,

on 20 June 1961, he testified that the measures taken toward the official "promotion of Zionism" in the late 1930s had aimed "to put the Jews on their feet in their own land" (Eichmann Trial records, The Nizkor Project, http://www.nizkor.org/hweb/people/e/eichmann-adolf/transcripts/Sessions/Session-075-07.html). A similar claim can already be found in a note Eichmann made in Argentina in 1956, "Meine Feststellugen zur Angelegenheit 'Judenfrage'" ("My statement on the matter of the 'Jewish question'"), which Arendt used: "ground under the feet of the Jews in any territory accessible to us" (Hannah Arendt Papers, Eichmann Trial, file 17, fol. 43; copy from the Library of Congress at the Hannah-Arendt-Zentrum at the University of Oldenburg; http://memory.loc.gov/mss/mharendt_pub/03/031590/0037.jpg). This claim was central to Eichmann's self-presentation, according to which he had always supported forced emigration as a less "bloody" solution to the Jewish question.

54. See *EJ*, 60, 62. In Berlin in March 1937, Eichmann established contact with a member of the Zionist underground organization, the Haganah, who lived in Palestine. This led to Eichmann receiving "a formal invitation to Palestine," which Heydrich decided he should accept. Eichmann and his superior at the time, Herbert Hagen, arrived in Haifa at the beginning of October 1937, but the enterprise turned out to be a failure. In 1938, when Eichmann was head of the Zentralstelle für Jüdische Auswanderung (Center for Emigration of Austrian Jews) in Vienna, there were further contacts between the SD and agents of Aliyah Beth, which arranged illegal immigration to Palestine. See Michael Wildt, ed., *Die Judenpolitik des SD 1935 bis 1938: Eine Dokumentation* (Munich: Oldenbourg, 1995), introduction, 43–44; Francis R. Nicosia, "Ein nützlicher Feind: Zionismus im nationalsozialistischen Deutschland 1933–1939," *Vierteljahrshefte für Zeitgeschichte* 37 (1989): 367–400, 397–398; Nicosia, *Zionism and Anti-Semitism in Nazi Germany* (Cambridge: Cambridge University Press, 2008).

55. An indication of the time of writing: a "quarter century" after the publication of Eichmann in Jerusalem (1963/64) points to the late 1980s.

56. At the University of Münster, in the summer term of 1975, Blumenberg lectured on the "theory of nonconceptuality" ("Theorie der Unbegrifflichkeit"); his 1979 book *Shipwreck with Spectator* includes a "Prospect for a Theory of Nonconceptuality." Both are connected to the resumption of Blumenberg's early project of metaphorology; now, metaphor, understood as thought and speech in images, was declared a special case of nonconceptuality, alongside myth. Cf. Hans Blumenberg, *Theorie der Unbegrifflichkeit*, ed. Anselm Haverkamp (Frankfurt: Suhrkamp, 2007). The intellectual leap from the claim that Arendt, the political scientist, had not understood (*Unbegreifen*) the identity, "verging on the inconceivable" (*am Rande des Unbegreiflichen*), of Nazi and Zionist interests in the question of emigration to Palestine, to the "theory of nonconceptuality" (*Unbegrifflichkeit*) is hard to follow. Only Blumenberg's subsequent interpretation of the Eichmann trial as a "mythical act" makes this connection understandable. [Blumenberg's rhetorical move, in the last two sentences of this paragraph, from *Unbegreiflichen* through *Unbegreifen* to *Unbegrifflichkeit*, is impossible to replicate in English. (Trans.)]

57. In the "Epilogue" to the Eichmann book, to which Blumenberg refers here, Arendt discussed the "legal problems that the trial inevitably posed." At the same,

time, however, she emphasized that there was no precedent for the crime of which Eichmann stood accused (*EJ*, 253).

58. Probably a reference to Arendt's criticisms of "the play aspect of the trial" (*EJ*, 6, 8). Blumenberg, by contrast, points to the historically unique event of the survivors of the Holocaust sitting in judgment, as the people of a state, over that crime's organizer.

59. As Blumenberg knew, the term "state of exception" was tainted by its association with Carl Schmitt. However, Karl Jaspers, in the debates of the 1960s surrounding the statute of limitation on Nazi crimes, also demanded that crimes committed in a "historical state of exception" should be subject to an "exceptional law." Karl Jaspers, *Wohin treibt die Bundesrepublik?* (Munich: Piper, 1966), 58–59, 62. [These passages are not included in the abridged English edition: Karl Jaspers, *The Future of Germany*, trans. and ed. E. B. Ashton with a foreword by Hannah Arendt (Chicago: University of Chicago Press, 1967). (Trans.)]

60. Attorney General Gideon Hausner, prosecuting, followed the historical-political intentions that David Ben Gurion had for the trial. Foremost among these was the proof of Eichmann's comprehensive responsibility for the planning and execution of the destruction of the European Jews. The accused was supposed to appear as a monstrous criminal on a large scale. At the same time, Hausner attempted to pin individual murders on Eichmann, but did not succeed.

61. I.e., the Nazi and Nazi Collaborators (Punishment) Law, which the Knesset had passed in August 1950 and in which standards of international law were applied to crimes against the Jewish people. Arendt found the law of 1950 to be unsuitable and insufficient to address the charges brought against Eichmann (*EJ*, 254, 263, 272). Cf. Jacob Robinson, *And the Crooked Shall Be Made Straight: The Eichmann Trial, the Jewish Catastrophe, and Hannah Arendt's Narrative* (New York: Macmillan, 1965), 87–88.

62. Arendt certainly did credit Eichmann with intelligence. Even before the trial, she wrote to Mary McCarthy on 20 June 1960 that "he was one of the most intelligent of the lot." Hannah Arendt and Mary McCarthy, *Between Friends: The Correspondence of Hannah Arendt and Mary McCarthy, 1949–1975*, ed. Carol Brightman (New York: Harcourt Brace, 1995), 81–82. That she later occasionally found Eichmann to be "stupid" does not refer to his intelligence, but points toward the concept of the "banality of evil"; see the afterword, p. 90, n. 45.

63. On the paterfamilias or family man, see above, p. 16, n. 34. Arendt gives the following assessment: "In court, Eichmann gave the impression of a typical member of the lower middle classes, and this impression was more than borne out by every sentence he spoke or wrote while in prison. But this was misleading, he was rather the déclassé son of a solid middle-class family" (*EJ*, 31).

64. A quotation from *EJ*, 35. Arendt reports Eichmann's testimony concerning his training in two Bavarian SS camps and his complaint about the "humdrum of military service," continuing: "Thus bored to distraction, he heard that the Security Service of the Reichsführer S.S. (Himmler's *Sicherheitsdienst*, or S.D., as I shall call it henceforth) had jobs open, and applied immediately."

65. Hannah Arendt drew a very dismissive picture of most of the prosecution witnesses (referred to by the trial authorities as "sufferings-of-the-Jewish-people

witnesses"), complaining that their testimonies stood in no obvious relation to the Eichmann case (*EJ*, 207–209).

66. Jehoshaphat (or Yehoshafat; Hebrew: "the Lord has judged"), the valley where, according to Joel 3:2 and 3:12, God would sit in judgment over his people's enemies. It has also been taken to represent the Last Judgment (e.g., Dante, *Inferno*, canto 10, line 11). The witnesses, Blumenberg seems to suggest, did not believe in the court in the Valley of Jehoshaphat, which is why they tried to turn the Jerusalem District Court into such a court, and blamed all their sufferings on Eichmann.

67. The Jerusalem District Court certainly did not sentence Eichmann for crimes that he did not, but might have, committed. Nevertheless, his counsel, Robert Servatius, argued that Eichmann was "a scapegoat [. . .] abandoned to the court in Jerusalem, contrary to international law," and Eichmann too, in his last statement, maintained his "profound conviction that [. . .] he must suffer for the acts of others." The Court of Appeal, however, did follow the prosecution's claims that Eichmann had been the initiator of the "final solution." See *EJ*, 247–249.

68. Arendt always insisted on judging Eichmann's guilt according to objective facts and not with reference to the crimes of others or even a supposed collective guilt. See *EJ*, 278; and also Arendt's lecture, "Personal Responsibility under Dictatorship" (1964), in Hannah Arendt, *Responsibility and Judgment*, ed. Jerome Kohn (New York: Schocken, 2003), 29.

69. Gershom Scholem had opposed the execution of Eichmann, fearing that it would make it easier for the Germans to come to terms with their past: "A great sigh of relief was heard in all the German press, and not only there, when the Israelis hanged Eichmann. He now stands for all and will remain standing as such." Arendt considered this a "fairy tale" and in any case not a compelling argument against the execution. Hannah Arendt, Gershom Scholem, *Der Briefwechsel*, ed. Marie Luise Knott (Berlin: Suhrkamp, 2010), 452, 459. In a television interview with Thilo Koch (1964), Arendt refuted claims made at the time against Nazi trials, and which had already been made against Eichmann's, "that this could only lead to finding scapegoats, at whose expense the German people could then collectively feel innocent." Hannah Arendt, *Ich will verstehen: Selbstauskünfte zu Leben und Werk*, ed. Ursula Ludz (Munich: Piper, 1996), 42.

70. Blumenberg subsumes Arendt's criticism of the Jerusalem trial and—as will be seen in the following—her definition of the Holocaust as a "crime against humanity" under the concept of "universal moralism" (or, later, "moral rigorism"). His counterargument, the "mythical necessity" of Eichmann's execution, makes its first appearance here.

71. A critical account of the German-Israeli reparations and compensation treaty of 1952, in which the Federal Republic undertook to pay compensation to Israel and to Jewish organizations, can be found in Tom Segev, *The Seventh Million: The Israelis and the Holocaust*, trans. Haim Watzman (New York: Henry Holt, 1991), pt. 4, pp. 189–254.

72. Blumenberg counted the intuitiveness (*Anschaulichkeit*) of myths among the reasons for their durability. The Jerusalem trial was thus a "mythical act" in concentrating all guilt for the suffering of the Jewish people on Eichmann. Only in this intuitiveness, not in the examination of social circumstances and

bureaucratically distributed responsibilities for the Holocaust, could the trial prove the legitimacy of the State of Israel. But Arendt, too, was aware that analyzing the bureaucracy of the Nazi state was little help in the courtroom; her concern, unlike Blumenberg's, was with the personal responsibility of the accused: "The Eichmann trial, like all such trials, would have been devoid of all interest if it had not transformed the cog or 'referent' of Section IV B4 in the Reich Security Head Office into a man." Arendt, "Personal Responsibility under Dictatorship," 31–32. [For the translation of *Anschauung* and derived terms, see the translator's note in Blumenberg, *Work on Myth*, 261: "[. . .] *Anschauung* means initially simple 'regarding' or viewing,' which is then elevated into a quasi-visual 'contemplation' or 'intuition' of a truth [. . .], and in these contexts the meaning does not have much to do with the usual nontechnical sense of 'intuition' as unusual, rationally inexplicable insight." (Trans.)]

73. Nowhere does Arendt make a general accusation of guilt against German society; on the contrary, she argued vehemently against the notion of collective guilt. However, she did emphasize, following the historian Raul Hilberg, "the complicity of all German offices and authorities in the Final Solution—of all civil servants in the state ministries, of the regular armed forces with their General Staff, of the judiciary, and of the business world" (*EJ*, 18). Besides, the notion constructed by German courts in the 1960s that the Holocaust was the work of a few "principal culprits" (Hitler, Himmler, Heydrich) led to the exculpation of countless accessories by a "judiciary of deputies" [*Gehilfen-Judikatur*, possibly a reference to Rolf Hochhuth's famous 1963 play *Der Gehilfe* (*The Deputy*) (Trans.)].

74. Earlier, Blumenberg noted: "It is a book [arguing] against Eichmann's sole guilt and for the responsibility of the Germans, at least insofar as their lag in atoning [for their crimes] is concerned. I do not disapprove of this tendency [. . .]." See below, p. 52.

75. "Analysis" refers to Arendt's supposedly sociological perspective. Though Blumenberg was far from considering irrelevant the question of who had made the "murderous bureaucrats" possible, it could not, in his view, be the object of a trial qua "mythical act."

76. In the aforementioned television interview with Günter Gaus, Arendt gave the following answer to the opening question: "I do not belong to the circle of philosophers. My profession, if one can even speak of it at all, is political theory. I neither feel like a philosopher, nor do I believe that I have been accepted in the circle of philosophers, as you so kindly suppose" ("'What Remains?,'" 3). In 1976, after Arendt's death, Hans Jonas sent a copy of his published eulogy, "Hannah Arendt as a Philosopher," to Blumenberg, who made the following note: "After Hannah Arendt had decided that she had done enough for political science and henceforth only to do *transpolitical things* [in English (Trans.)], around 1974, in unison with Jonas: 'It's now or never.'" The note is entitled "ESCHAT [eschatology] The shortest formula for the state of exception." Index card 17253, card file 4, DLA Marbach, Nachlass Hans Blumenberg.

77. The charge of rigorism, which was first made, by analogy with Freud, against Arendt's claim to truth, is now leveled at Arendt the moralist. Blumenberg is likely to have had Arendt's unjustified criticism of the conduct of the *Judenräte* in mind.

78. In Blumenberg's reading, Arendt's own dilemma consisted in the irreconcilability of two of her book's tendencies: the banalization of Eichmann, on the one hand, and her call for an international tribunal, on the other (see below, p. 24, n. 81). But Blumenberg is mistaken if he supposes Arendt to have seen Eichmann "degraded before all eyes" to a "buffoon" or "clown"; in fact, she thought he was an actual clown, which is no less problematic. In the crucial passage, Arendt discussed "the dilemma between the unspeakable horror of the deeds and the undeniable ludicrousness of the man who perpetrated them" before continuing: "Despite all the efforts of the prosecution, everybody could see that this man was not a 'monster,' but it was difficult indeed not to suspect that he was a clown" (*EJ*, 54). In the interview with Günter Gaus, she puts this yet more bluntly: "I was really of the opinion that Eichmann was a buffoon. I'll tell you this: I read the transcript of his police investigation, thirty-six hundred pages, read it, and read it very carefully, and I do not know how many times I laughed—laughed out loud!" ("'What Remains?,'" 15)—Eichmann's cross-examination by the Israeli police captain Avner Less on 5 July 1960, which addressed his role among the high-ranking participants of the Wannsee Conference, contains a statement that suggests that Arendt took Eichmann, whose defense strategy was to downplay his own authority, at his word: "[. . .] then Heydrich could have said: what's more, for particular cases, talk to Obersturmbannführer Eichmann here—he could after all have said that—but he didn't. I was far too small a clown—please—let's put that in quotation marks this time—I was—never mind the quotation marks—because they were all by and large Obergruppenführer and Gruppenführer, all in a general's rank." Quoted in Kurt Pätzold and Erika Schwarz, *Tagesordnung: Judenmord* (Berlin: Metropol, 1992), 178–179. [Jochen von Lang, ed., *Eichmann Interrogated: Transcripts from the Archives of the Israeli Police* (New York: Farrar, Straus and Giroux, 1983), does not reproduce this passage. (Trans.)] See also Bettina Stangneth, "Eichmanns Erzählungen," in *Die Wannsee-Konferenz am 20. Januar 1942: Dokumente, Forschungsstand, Kontroversen*, ed. Norbert Kampe and Peter Klein (Cologne: Böhlau, 2013), 138–150, 146–147.

79. A reference to the judgment Arendt herself composed (*EJ*, 277–279).

80. This sentence is a close paraphrase of Arendt's judgment: "[. . .] as though you and your superiors had any right to determine who should and who should not inhabit the world—we find that no one, that is, no member of the human race, can be expected to want to share the earth with you" (*EJ*, 279).

81. Arendt's point of departure was the definition of "crimes against humanity" based on the London (or Nuremberg) Charter of August 1945, which was first applied in the Nuremberg Trials. The charge against Eichmann, on the other hand, was principally one of "crimes against the Jewish people." Arendt wished to see underscored the novelty and unprecedentedness of the crime the Jews had fallen victim to. Her call for an international tribunal, in which she concurred with Karl Jaspers, was an expression of this wish: "Insofar as the victims were Jews, it was right and proper that a Jewish court should sit in judgment; but insofar as the crime was a crime against humanity, it needed an international tribunal to do justice to it" (*EJ*, 269; see also 254, 267). But she also called her own demand into question: One must not forget what it meant, she wrote, "that, for the first time (since the year 70, when Jerusalem was destroyed by the Romans), Jews were able to sit

in judgment on crimes committed against their own people, that, for the first time, they did not need to appeal to others for protection and justice, or fall back upon the compromised phraseology of the rights of man—rights which, as no one knew better than they, were claimed only by people who were too weak to defend their 'rights as Englishmen' and to enforce their own laws. (The very fact that Israel had her own law under which such a trial could be held had been called, long before the Eichmann trial, an expression of 'a evolutionary transformation that has taken place in the political position of the Jewish people'—by [Pinhas] Rosen on the occasion of the First Reading of the Law in 1950 in the Knesset)" (*EJ*, 271–272). This position is not that far from Blumenberg's, although Arendt had recourse not to a "myth," but to the historical experience of the Jewish people.

82. A reference to the charge of cooperation between Jewish functionaries and Nazis brought by Arendt. She also mentioned the kapo system in the concentration camps and the work of the "Jewish commandos" at Auschwitz, concluding, somewhat implausibly, that "a clear-cut division between persecutors and victims" could not be upheld (*EJ*, 120). [The term "kapo system" does not appear in the English edition, but in *EJG*, 156. (Trans.)] In an earlier version, which hints at the very personal background to his argument, Blumenberg wrote: "Much worse is that Hannah Arendt gives the victims themselves a share in the blame for their doom. Historically justified, but from the distance of one who does not know what it means to want to save one's skin [. . .]." See below, p. 48.

83. Blumenberg explains the charge that Arendt was "apolitical" further on, claiming that she had failed "to recognize the public and political status of the trial."

84. The Last Judgment in a terrestrial form.

85. In the session of 17 April 1961, Eichmann pleaded not guilty to all charges and repeatedly stated throughout the trial that he "felt free of all guilt." Cf. Arendt's point: "Foremost among the larger issues at stake in the Eichmann trial was the assumption current in all modern legal systems that intent to do wrong is necessary for the commission of a crime" (*EJ*, 277). Blumenberg, on the other hand, emphasizes that personal guilt and thus a "punishment" requiring proof of culpability could precisely not have been the concerns of the Jerusalem court. Under this condition, Eichmann's execution could not but take on the character of a ritual.

86. Following Eichmann's execution on 31 May 1962, his body was cremated and the ashes scattered over the Mediterranean Sea.

87. Arendt quotes the American constitutional lawyer Yosal Rogat, who had written an early study of the Eichmann trial: "[. . .] that a great crime offends nature, so that the very earth cries out for vengeance; that evil violates a natural harmony which only retribution can restore; and that a wronged collectivity owes a duty to the moral order to punish the criminal." Yosal Rogat, *The Eichmann Trial and the Rule of Law* (Santa Barbara, CA: Center for the Study of Democratic Institutions, 1961), 22. She added her own commentary: "And yet [. . .] it was precisely on the basis of these long-forgotten propositions that Eichmann was brought to justice to begin with, and that they were, in fact, the supreme justification for the death penalty. Because he had been implicated and had played a central role in an enterprise whose only purpose was to eliminate forever certain 'races' from the surface of the earth, he had to be eliminated. And if it is true that 'justice must

not only be done but must be seen to be done' [Rogat, *Eichmann Trial*, 34], then the justice of what was done in Jerusalem would have emerged to be seen by all if the judges had dared to address their defendant in something like the following terms: [. . .]" (*EJ*, 277; there follows Arendt's own proposed verdict). The passage leaves no doubt that Arendt did not reject Rogat's line of thought—the "long-forgotten propositions"—but rather adopted it, in order to connect it to her own proposed justification of the death sentence, that "he could no longer remain on earth among human beings" (*EJG*, 327; no exact counterpart in *EJ*). A textual comparison confirms this. Immediately preceding the passage quoted by Arendt, Rogat argues that penal ideas from times long past could help us understand the Eichmann trial: "Finally, attitudes toward punishment also follow from this older outlook; and, once again, perceiving them helps us to understand the trial. There was a time long ago when our questions about the appropriateness of the trial would not have been raised because the following propositions were accepted: that a great crime offends nature, so that the very earth cries out for vengeance [. . .]" (Rogat, *Eichmann Trial*, 22). Arendt's adaptation of this idea produced the following passage: "We refuse, and consider as barbaric, the proposition, 'that a great crime offends nature [. . .].' And yet I think it is undeniable that it was precisely on the basis of these long-forgotten propositions that Eichmann was brought to justice [. . .]" (*EJ*, 277). Brigitte Granzow's draft translation into German stayed very close to the original phrasing ("Wir lehnen die Auffassung ab, betrachten sie gar als barbarisch [. . .]"). The version to which Blumenberg refers came about through an amendment by Arendt's own hand: "All das sind für uns antiquierte Vorstellungen, die wir als barbarisch ablehnen" (All these are to us long-forgotten propositions [more literally: antiquated notions], which we reject as barbaric). Hannah Arendt Papers, *Eichmann in Jerusalem*, German translation, corrected draft, copy from the Library of Congress at the Hannah-Arendt-Zentrum at the University of Oldenburg; online at http://memory.loc.gov/mss/mharendt_pub/05/050310/0036.jpg.

88. The legal principle of retaliation, to repay like with like. Arendt did not see vengeance at work, but was afraid that Attorney General Hausner's rather pathos-laden delivery of the case for the prosecution would prove right all those who argued that "the trial [. . .] was established not in order to satisfy the demands of justice but to still the victims' desire for and, perhaps, right to vengeance" (*EJ*, 260–261).

89. See above, p. 17, n. 35.

90. The television interview makes no direct mention of a supposed "lack of piety toward the victims," but Gaus did ask Arendt, with reference to Scholem's charge against her: "Is the criticism that your book is lacking in love for the Jewish people painful to you?" Arendt's reply was evasive ("'What Remains?,'" 15–17; cf. Arendt/Scholem, *Briefwechsel*, 429, 439–440). When Blumenberg, in the 1970s, made notes on this interview and, in doing so, began to frame a critique of Arendt, the lack of "love for the Jews," of which Scholem had complained, became "a lack of piety toward the victims" (see below, p. 47). In doing so, he may have been guided by Arendt's admission that "the tone of voice is predominantly ironic" ("'What Remains?,'" 16).

91. Probably a reference to the gap between a legal and a political assessment of the Eichmann trial.

92. The phrase *hätten wünschen müssen* is ambiguous, conveying both descriptive and prescriptive meanings. (Trans.)

93. A possible reference to Hitler's so-called Nero order (Nerobefehl) of March 1945 and his remarks to Albert Speer: "Hitler told him coldly that should the war be lost, the [German] people would also be lost, and that there was no necessity of taking consideration of the basis even of its most primitive survival." Ian Kershaw, *Hitler 1936–45: Nemesis* (London: Penguin, 2001), 785. See also *Der Prozeß gegen die Hauptkriegsverbrecher vor dem Internationalen Militärgerichtshof Nürnberg* (Nuremberg: Internationaler Militärgerichtshof, 1947–49), 41:428–429, 430.

94. It is as impossible to determine the moment at which Hitler was "undemonized"—and that must also mean, in this context, seen as a "figure of ridicule"—as it is to prove the counterfactual supposition that this would not have happened if the Germans had put him on trial and sentenced him to death. The turn away from a Hitler-centric approach to history began, in Germany, in the 1970s and 1980s, and was driven above all by exponents of a functionalist interpretation of the Nazi regime. In doing so, the historian Hans Mommsen developed the controversial idea of Hitler as a "weak dictator." For a summary of these debates, see Ian Kershaw, *The Nazi Dictatorship: Problems and Perspectives of Interpretation*, 4th ed. (London: Bloomsbury, 2000), chap. 4.

95. Elsewhere, in the context of reflections on the divergence of "appearance" and "significance," Blumenberg stated that it was a sign of realism "to be able to cope with surprises like that of Eichmann's features being those of an accountant rather than of a larger-than-life monster." Hans Blumenberg, *Beschreibung des Menschen*, ed. Manfred Sommer (Frankfurt: Suhrkamp, 2006), 688.

96. In a 1964 interview with Joachim Fest, with which Blumenberg was probably not familiar, Arendt said: "[. . .] if there was ever anyone who deprived himself of any demonic aura, it was Herr Eichmann." "Eichmann Was Outrageously Stupid," interview with Joachim Fest (1964), in Hannah Arendt, *The Last Interview and Other Conversations* (New York: Melville House, 2013), 39–65, 46. She made a similar statement to Thilo Koch (*Ich will verstehen*, 40). Already during the trial, Arendt had written to Jaspers on 13 April 1961: "Eichmann is no eagle; rather, a ghost who [. . .] minute by minute fades in substance, as it were, in his glass box" (Arendt and Jaspers, *Correspondence*, 434).

97. Blumenberg here refers to Adelbert Reif, ed., *Gespräche mit Hannah Arendt* (Munich: Piper, 1976), 9–34, 26. This corresponds to the interview with Günter Gaus cited above ("'What Remains?,'" 15): "I was really of the opinion that Eichmann was a buffoon. I'll tell you this: I read the transcript of his police investigation, thirty-six hundred pages, read it, and read it very carefully, and I do not know how many times I laughed—laughed out loud! People took this reaction in a bad way." [Note that *buffoon* is the (perhaps more apposite) reverse translation of *Hanswurst*, the term used for the original *clown* in the authorized German translation of *Eichmann in Jerusalem*. (Trans.)] See also above, p. 24, n. 78.

98. In discussing, with Günter Gaus, possible reasons for keeping quiet about a recognized truth, Arendt explained: "But look here, someone asked me, if I had anticipated one thing or another, would I have written the Eichmann book

differently? I answered: No. I would have confronted the alternative: to write or not to write. Because one can also hold one's tongue" ("'What Remains?,'" 18).

99. Freud, *Totem and Taboo* (*SE*, 13:140–146); Freud, *Moses and Monotheism* (*SE*, 23:37).

100. In describing the Holocaust as a "massacre," Blumenberg situates it in the history of comparable atrocities; Arendt, on the other hand, always emphasized the historic novelty of these "administrative massacres" planned by the state. The phrase is to be found in Arendt's preface to the German edition (*EJG*, 17; cf. *EJ*, 267), where Eichmann's crime is described as "unprecedented" and Auschwitz as a "horror [. . .] of a different nature from all the atrocities of the past."

# II

# EXCERPTS AND PRELIMINARY STUDIES

**On Sigmund Freud, *Moses and Monotheism***

Moses the Egyptian[1]

Moses, the Egyptian of pharaonic blood, was invented by Sigmund Freud as a blow to his people. It was the last of his acts, the entirety of which he himself conceived of as a 'blow' to mankind and with which he saw himself in the succession of Copernicus and Darwin in sobering the species. Freud belongs to the great enlighteners, who consider the hardness of their discipline, practiced in the profession

---

1. Undated typescript, collection [*Konvolut*] "Text- und Materialsammlung Moses der Ägypter." All excerpts and preliminary studies reproduced here are held at DLA Marbach, Nachlass Hans Blumenberg. Unless otherwise indicated, titles and short bibliographic references in the text are Blumenberg's, while footnotes are the editor's.

of science and maintained for a lifetime, to be everybody's business or who want to make it everybody's business: causing man to be shocked at himself would keep him from new illusions. He was one of those whose trust in truth is limitless, however deep it may cast us; loving the truth that would set us free allows one to expect everything of oneself and of others. It was supposed to be the great and ultimate antidote to prejudice, to lodge science not just in the minds but also in the hearts of men. Precisely that has failed, and this failure is the result of the last two centuries, [a result] whose consequences cannot yet be estimated. Perhaps it is also the result of the hardness that was almost taken for granted in the 'education of humankind' by science. Freud, who intended to liberate men from one of its greatest constraints, thought nothing of placing upon them the burden of the truth about themselves and having them gaze into their abysses in countless hours of analysis across the world.

Bearing this in mind, it remains[2] dismaying what Freud did in 1939 with "Moses and Monotheism."

Freud on the Creation of the Jew [excerpt][3]

*S. Freud to Arnold Zweig, 30.IX.1934*[4] Faced with the new persecutions, one asks oneself again how the Jews have come to be what they are and why they have attracted this undying hatred. I soon discovered the formula: Moses created the Jews. So I gave my work the title: *The Man Moses, a historical novel* (with more justification than your Nietzsche novel). The material fits into three sections. The first part is like an interesting novel; the second is laborious and boring; the third is full of content and

---

2. Blumenberg amended the original version, "it is no longer so dismaying," by hand to read "it remains."

3. Index cards 8680–8681 [1964], JDT [Judentum], box 5.

4. Blumenberg excerpted this passage from the first edition of Sigmund Freud, *Briefe 1873–1939* (Frankfurt: Fischer, 1960), 414f. The translation reproduced here follows that in *Letters of Sigmund Freud and Arnold Zweig*, 91–92. Emphases in the letters added by Blumenberg. (Trans.)

makes exciting reading. The whole enterprise broke down on this third section, for it involved a theory of religion—certainly nothing new for me after *Totem and Taboo*, but something new and fundamental for the uninitiated. It is the thought of these uninitiated readers that makes me *hold over the finished work*. For we live here in an atmosphere of Catholic orthodoxy. They say *that the politics of our country are determined by one Pater Schmidt*, who lives in St. Gabriel near Mödling. He is a confidant of the Pope, and makes no secret of his abhorrence of analysis and especially of my totem theory. My good friend Edoardo Weiss has founded a psychoanalytical group in Rome and published several numbers of a *Rivista Italiana di Psicoanalisis*. Suddenly this publication was prohibited and although Weiss had direct access to Mussolini and had received a promise of help from him, the ban could not be lifted. It is said to have come direct from the Vatican and Pater Schmidt to have been responsible for it. Now, any publication of mine will be sure to attract a certain amount of attention, which will not escape the notice of this inimical priest. Thus we might be risking a ban on psychoanalysis in Vienna and the suspension of all our publications here.

*S. Freud to Anonymous, 14.XII.1937*[5] Several years ago I started asking myself how the Jews acquired their particular character, and following my usual custom I went back to the earliest beginnings. I did not get far. I was astounded to find that already *the first so to speak embryonic experience* of the race, the influence of the man Moses and the exodus from Egypt, conditioned the entire further development up to the present day— *like a regular trauma of early childhood* in the case history of a neurotic individual. To begin with, there is the temporal conception of life and the conquest of magic thought, the rejection of mysticism, both of which can be traced back to Moses himself

---

5. *Letters of Sigmund Freud*, 439.

and—although not with all the historical certainty that could be desired—perhaps a little further.

### The Historical Novel "The Man Moses" and the Consequences [excerpt][6]

*Sigmund Freud to Arnold Zweig, Vienna, 30 September 1934.*[7] *On the origins of "The Man Moses"* "Faced with the new persecutions, one asks oneself again how the Jews have come to be what they are and why they have attracted this undying hatred. I soon discovered the formula: *Moses created the Jews.* So I gave my work the title: *The Man Moses, a historical novel* (with more justification than your Nietzsche novel). The material fits into three sections. The first part is like an interesting novel; the second is laborious and boring; the third is full of content and makes exciting reading. The whole enterprise broke down on this third section, for it involved a *theory of religion*—certainly nothing new for me after *Totem and Taboo*, but something new and fundamental for the uninitiated. It is the thought of these uninitiated readers that makes me hold over the finished work. For we live here in an atmosphere of Catholic orthodoxy. They say that the politics of our country are determined by one *Pater Schmidt* . . . Thus we might be risking a ban on psychoanalysis in Vienna and the suspension of all our publications here. If this danger involved me alone, I would be but little concerned, but to deprive all our members in Vienna of their livelihood is too great a responsibility. And in addition there is the fact that this work does not seem to me sufficiently substantiated, nor does it altogether please me. It is therefore *not the occasion for a martyrdom.* Enough of this for the moment." (The first part of the book appeared in 1937, the rest in 1939.)

---

6. Index cards 16305–16308 [1975], ANTHR [Anthropologie] FREUD, card file 1.

7. *Letters of Sigmund Freud and Arnold Zweig*, 91–92.

*Sigmund Freud to Arnold Zweig, Vienna, 6 November 1934*[8] "But the risk, though real enough,[9] is not the only obstacle. More important is the fact that *this historical novel won't stand up to my own criticism*. I need more certainty and I should not like to endanger the final formula of the whole book, which I regard as valuable, by founding it on a base of clay.[10] So let us leave it aside."

*Sigmund Freud to Arnold Zweig, Vienna, 16 December 1934*[11] "Don't say any more about the Moses book. The fact that this, probably *my last creative effort, should have come to grief* depresses me enough as it is. Not that I can shake him off. The man and what I wanted to make of him pursue me everywhere. But it would not do; the external dangers and inner misgivings allow of no other solution . . . Nor is it any inner uncertainty on my part, for *that is as good as settled*, but that fact that I was obliged to construct so imposing a statue upon feet of clay, so that *any fool could topple it*."

*Sigmund Freud to Arnold Zweig, Vienna, 13 February 1935*[12] "Nothing can be done about my *Moses* . . . I shall send back your *Schöpfungsgedicht* [creation poem (reference unclear)] . . . It seems to me to pay too much respect to the *barbarous god of volcanoes and wildernesses* whom I grew to dislike very much in the course of my studies in Moses and who *was quite alien to my Jewish consciousness*. In my text I maintain that *the hero Moses had never heard the name Yahweh* . . ."

*Sigmund Freud to Arnold Zweig, Vienna, 15 March 1935*[13] "The misunderstanding of Egyptian pre-history in Israel's religious development is just as great in Auerbach as in the Biblical tradition. Even their famous historical and literary sense can only be an Egyptian legacy."

---

8. Ibid., 97. [The erroneous transcriptions from Freud's original letters are carried over into English from the German editions. (Trans.)]

9. *Real genug*, actually *real gering* (in reality small) in Freud's original letter.

10. *Tönerne Basis*, actually *höhere Basis* (higher foundation) in Freud's original letter.

11. *Letters of Sigmund Freud and Arnold Zweig*, 98.

12. Ibid., 102.

13. Ibid., 105.

*Sigmund Freud to Arnold Zweig, Vienna, 2 May 1935*[14] "Moses will not let go of my imagination. I picture myself reading it aloud to you when you come to Vienna, despite my defective speech. In an account of Tel el Amarna, which has not yet been fully excavated, I noticed a comment on a certain Prince Thothmes, of whom nothing further is known. If I were a millionaire,[15] I would finance the continuation of these excavations. *Thothmes could be my Moses* and I would be able to boast that I had guessed right."

*Sigmund Freud to Arnold Zweig, Vienna, 13 June 1935*[16] "As far as my own productivity goes, it is like what happens in analysis. If a particular subject has been suppressed, nothing takes its place and the field of vision remains empty. So do I now *remain fixated on the Moses*, which has been laid aside and on which I can do no more."

*Sigmund Freud to Arnold Zweig, Vienna, 20 January 1936*[17] "So there is little hope of rousing my Moses in this way from the sleep which is his destiny."

*Sigmund Freud to Arnold Zweig, Vienna, 17 June 1936*[18] "I gladly accept your offer of a list of writers who acknowledged Moses to be an Egyptian. But not one of them has made anything of the fact. *Thomas Mann*, who delivered his lecture on me in five or six different places, was kind enough to repeat it for me personally in my room here in Grinzing on Sunday 14th. This was a great joy for me and for all my family who were present."

*Sigmund Freud to Arnold Zweig, Vienna, 20 December 1937*[19] "I will be sending a copy of *Moses* to you before the year is up. It will

---

14. Ibid., 106.
15. *Fund-Millionär*, actually *Pfund-Millionär* (millionaire in Pounds [Sterling]) in Freud's original letter.
16. *Letters of Sigmund Freud and Arnold Zweig*, 107.
17. Ibid., 119.
18. Ibid., 131.
19. Ibid., 154.

certainly cause a stir in a world that is hungry for sensation. Several offers from America and even from England to publish a *Psychoanalysis of the Bible* with the appropriate firms . . ."

*Sigmund Freud to Arnold Zweig, London, 5 March 1939*[20]
"I cannot imagine what 'consoling explanations' you have discovered in my *Civilization and its Discontents*. Nowadays this book has become very remote to me. I am only waiting for Moses, which is due to appear in March, and then I need not be interested in any book of mine again until my next reincarnation."

[Typewritten addition:] Must one not compare Husserl's 'Crisis' treatise and Freud's 'Moses'? Galileo in one with Moses in the other? Their false gods? Their final explanations for calamity [*Unheil*]?

Not Enough Culture to Be Sufficiently Discontented with It. Horace's *Impavidus* Is Narcissism Typified[21]

*Freud, discussion remarks (K 15447.64, 215)*[22] On March 20, 1930, the topic of the meeting was Freud's monograph "Civilization and Its Discontents." He himself was very critical of his own work. The structure was a failure, but one did not make the structure of a book oneself, it made itself, and if one struggled against writing accordingly, the outcome was unknowable.

But above all, the book had a defect that had remained altogether unnoticed by others: "None of you has noted one omission in the work, and this is a gigantic disgrace. I myself noticed it only after the book was already printed. *My* omission is excusable, but not yours. I had good reason to forget something that I know very distinctly. If I had not forgotten it, but had written it down, it would have been unbearable."

---

20. Ibid., 78.
21. Two index cards, no dating possible [ca. 1980], ANTHR FREUD, card file 1.
22. Coded source: Richard Sterba, "Unpublizierte Diskussionsbemerkungen Sigmund Freuds," *Jahrbuch der Psychoanalyse* 10 (1978): 214–216, on 215. Freud's words are reproduced here according to Sterba, *Reminiscences of a Viennese Psychoanalyst*, 114–116.

To introduce what he meant to say, Freud quoted the two verses from Horace, which he also translated himself: "If the firmament should break to pieces over him, / the fragments will bury a fearless man." As Bultmann had even altered the Latin text of these two verses,[23] so Freud changes their meaning: the fearless man whom Horace sees before him is the stoic by dint of his own inner moral strength, whereas Freud reads in him narcissism typified: "This possibility of happiness is so very sad. It is the person who relies completely upon himself. A caricature of this type is Falstaff. We can tolerate him as a caricature, but otherwise he is unbearable. This is the absolute narcissist. The unassailability by anything is given only to the absolute narcissist. My omission is a real defect in the presentation."

It does not sit well with this misunderstanding that Freud sees man in the face of apocalyptic threats as a stoic, too, even in this year 1930 no longer taking seriously resistance to his own teachings: "During my whole life I have endeavored to uncover truths. I had no other intention and everything else was completely a matter of indifference to me. My single motive was the love of truth. It does no harm to anybody. You can unconcernedly tell people the worst. If we were told that a comet will destroy our planet in one hundred fifty years, nobody would let this announcement disturb him from enjoying his breakfast. The death of each of you is certain, mine obviously in a shorter time, and you do not let yourself be disturbed by this. Seven years ago I was told that I would have a maximum of five years to live, and since I talk it rather well, I can also tell mankind the most unpleasant things; it does not touch them." Then Freud made a pronouncement which might be called classical: "Actually, the truth is that we do not have so much culture that we could really feel uncomfortable in it."

---

23. Cf. Blumenberg's review of Rudolf Bultmann, *Geschichte und Eschatologie, Gnomon* 31, no. 2 (1959): 163–166; see also typescript ESC [Eschatologie] X, fols. 23ff., DLA Marbach, Nachlass Hans Blumenberg.

## Behaving like the Father of the Primal Horde[24]

*Fritz Wittels, Sigmund Freud (Leipzig, 1924), 122*   In spring 1910, the Second Congress of Psychoanalysts was held in Nuremberg, after the First [Congress in] 1908 in Salzburg. Ferenczi proposed a motion that an international association should be founded, whose president for life was to be Jung: "He was to receive absolute power over appointing and dismissing analysts." All publications were to be subject to his approval. The bewilderment of the unsuspecting Viennese group: "I do not know whether such a thing has ever been thought up outside a Catholic order . . . Freud behaved like the father of Darwin's primal horde: just as violently and just as naively" (123).[25] He found no majority for this plan. "On the afternoon of this momentous day, the Viennese gentlemen gathered in a smaller room of the Nuremberg Grand Hotel to discuss the extraordinary situation. Suddenly, Freud appeared uninvited among them. He was highly agitated, as I have never seen him, and said: 'Most of you are Jews and hence not suited to winning friends for our new teaching. Jews must be content to be fertilizers of culture. I must keep up with science; am an old man, am tired of the hostility. We are all of us in danger.' He grasped his frock coat by the lapels: '*I will not even be left with this coat*,' he said. 'The Swiss will save us. Me and all of you.'"

This is what Clark's new biography of Freud has to say on this matter: "Now, a quarter of a century after Freud had so eagerly recruited Jung as a defense against the charge that psychoanalysis was a Jewish development, the final solution to the question was emerging. Jung was now 'proving' that psychoanalysis was Jewish."[26]

This refers to a letter that Freud had written in June 1934 to C. E. Benda, in which he protested against the charge of being

---

24. Index cards 21968–21959 [1981], ANTHR FREUD, card file 1.
25. Cf. Hans Blumenberg, *Höhlenausgänge* (Frankfurt: Suhrkamp, 1989), 693.
26. Ronald W. Clark, *Freud: The Man and the Cause* (New York: Random House, 1980), 494.

an anti-Semite. This was supposedly put about by the Freudians, "thereby confirming every time that psychoanalysis is in fact a Jewish psychology which nobody else can criticize without making himself guilty of anti-Semitism."[27] In this question, too, Freud had backed the wrong horse, just as he explained to a visitor, as late as 1937, that *he was not afraid of the Nazis, his true enemy was religion*.[28] To Arnold Zweig he further explained on the subject that it was above all the Viennese ethnological school of Wilhelm Schmidt that was his principal opponent.

Last Word on Nazi Barbarism[29]

*Arthur Koestler, Die Geheimschrift: Bericht eines Lebens 1932–1940 (Munich, 1954), 436*[30] In the autumn of 1938, Koestler visits Freud in London to ask him for a contribution to "Die Zukunft," which is planning an Anglo-German special edition. Koestler tries to get Freud to comment on events in Germany. His records of the conversation are lost, he reconstructs its gist at a great delay, and it won't be altogether wide of the mark:

"Well, you know, they [the Nazis] are *abreacting* the aggression pent up in our civilisation. Something like this was inevitable, sooner or later. I am not sure that from my standpoint I can blame them."

Which is to say: Unfortunately, I find myself in possession of a theory that puts me in the awkward position of being unable to

---

27. Ibid.; see also Carl Gustav Jung, *Letters*, vol. 1, *1906–1950*, ed. Gerhard Adler and trans. R. F. C. Hull (Princeton, NJ: Princeton University Press, 1973), 167. (Trans.)

28. "'The Nazis? I am not afraid of them. Help me rather to combat my true enemy.' Astonished, I asked him just which enemy was in question, and I heard him reply: 'Religion, the Roman Catholic Church.'" René Laforgue, "Personal Memories of Freud," in *Freud as We Knew Him*, ed. Hendrik M. Ruitenbeek (Detroit: Wayne State University Press, 1973), 344. (Trans.)

29. Index cards 22759–22760 [1982], ANTHR FREUD, collection "Text und Materialsammlung Moses der Ägypter."

30. Translation of Arthur Koestler, *The Invisible Writing: The Second Volume of an Autobiography, 1932–40* (1954) (London: Vintage, 2005), 67. (Trans.)

pass censure on what, according to this theory, happened inevitably and will happen again at any time. The stoic is not quite so free as befits such [a man]; he finds himself in the sticky situation of having not only fearlessly to let the world collapse over him, but also to deliver a commentary on the necessity [of its doing so]. That is the fate of those who make such good theories that their by-product is a philosophy of history capable of explaining what has happened and what is happening, but which in doing so prohibits any moral judgment.

In 1921, in the study "Group Psychology and the Analysis of the Ego," Freud had made a connection between the phenomenon of the group and his reconstruction of prehistory and found in this primal scene, discovered a decade previously, the two poles of the relationship between group and leader: "Thus the group appears to us as a revival of the primitive horde. Just as primitive man survives potentially in every individual so the primal horde may arise once more out of any random collection [. . .]."[31] But also the figure that alone is adequate to the group, that of the individual as the one who alone has the right to subjugate it: "He, at the very beginning of the history of mankind, was the 'superman' whom Nietzsche only expected from the future."[32] He—that is the father of the primal horde with his unrestricted power of chastisement, but also with the risk of being killed by the conspiracy of the chastised.[33]

---

31. Freud, *Group Psychology and the Analysis of the Ego*, in *SE*, 18:123.
32. Ibid.
33. See also index card 21819, ANTHR FREUD, card file 1, which is entitled "The dead Freud on the wanted list for Hitler's operation 'Seelöwe' [the planned invasion of the British Isles (Trans.)]." The card bears the following typewritten addition: "One must bear in mind what the Freud said of the last months of his life to A. Koestler (*The Invisible Writing*) about the N[ational] S[ocialists]: eruption of civilizationally pent-up aggression—[he was] not even sure if he could condemn the barbaric phenomenon, which of course means he sees it as a determinist natural event, [stemming] from the unbearableness of culture, from the discontents of civilization."

First Overestimation of "Moses and Monotheism"
in Vienna—Then Underestimation of the
Consolation Denied in London[34]

*Freud to Arnold Zweig, 30 September 1934* "Moses the Egyptian," the first part of what was to become "Moses and Monotheism," first appeared in 1937 in "Imago." Freud had delayed publication out of concern for the situation of psychoanalysis in Austria, where Wilhelm Schmidt in particular had been unable to forgive Freud "Totem and Taboo." It was too great a responsibility for him, he wrote to Zweig, to make unemployed all members of the association active in Vienna. But that the obligation toward truth could not be brought to bear against this hesitation, Freud moderates the historical content, the historical stringency of his thesis: "It is therefore not the occasion for a martyrdom."

Then, when after the occupation of Vienna, consideration for the much-demonized Wilhelm Schmidt no longer mattered, Freud had a new consideration in view, which, however, he no longer intended to respect: "With the audacity of one who has little or nothing left to lose";[35] this new consideration was given the English, whom Freud refers to as "my new compatriots" and among whom, easily wounded in their biblical learning, he could only lose the sympathy he had been so freely offered. But after all, in the book edition he also mentions that Jews from America and Palestine, as well as Christians concerned with the state of his soul, had visited him at his London house to ask him not to publish the work.[36] Among them had been communications that had wanted to direct him upon the ways of Christ "and sought to enlighten me

---

34. Index cards 22761–22762 [1982], ANTHR FREUD, collection "Text und Materialsammlung Moses der Ägypter." In a note, Blumenberg recapitulated the contents of these cards as follows: "Self-misjudgment of 'Moses and Monotheism' first in Vienna, then in London, terrible miscalculation of the consolation denied his own people." See fig. 1, p. 67.

35. The phrase is from the first prefatory note to the last part of *Moses and Monotheism*, which Freud wrote, according to his statements, before March 1938 and hence still in Vienna (*SE*, 23:54).

36. In the second prefatory note of June 1938, Freud mentions no visits from Jews from America or Palestine asking him not to publish the work (*SE*, 23:57–58).

on the future of Israel."[37] In the letter to Arnold Zweig of 28 June 1938, such a concern is explicitly mentioned. From America, Freud had received a letter from a Jew, "imploring me not to deprive our poor unhappy people of the one consolation remaining to them in their misery."[38] All Freud sees in this is the overestimation of a dry study, as if by such means one could destroy a faith. Did he honestly mean that? And was that even the question? And if one could not do so—what was the worth of all that Freud had written on the critique of religion in the last decade?

[Typewritten addition:] No, this is the narcissism of the father of the school, who pays anxious attention to the dangers of Wilhelm Schmidt, then ignores the dangers of Hitler (cf. the interview with Koestler!).

## On Hannah Arendt, *Eichmann in Jerusalem*

The Paterfamilias in the Organization of Murder [excerpt][1]

*Hannah Arendt, "Organisierte Schuld," Die Wandlung, vol. 1, no. 4*[2] "In trying to understand what were the real motives which caused people to act as cogs in the mass-murder machine, we shall not be aided by speculations about German history and the so-called German national character, of whose potentialities those who knew Germany most intimately had not the slightest idea fifteen years ago. There is more to be learned from the characteristic personality of the man who can boast that he was the organizing spirit of the murder. Heinrich Himmler . . . is neither a Bohemian like Goebbels, nor a sex criminal like Streicher, nor

---

37. *SE*, 23:57.
38. Jones, *Life and Work*, 3:250; the quotation can be found in *Letters of Sigmund Freud and Arnold Zweig*, 163.
1. Index cards 518–520 [1946], Gegenwart, collection "Text- und Materialsammlung Moses der Ägypter."
2. This is the version from which Blumenberg quotes. The text reproduced here follows that of "Organized Guilt and Universal Responsibility" (1945), in *Portable Hannah Arendt*, 146–156, 151–154.

a perverted fanatic like Hitler, nor an adventurer like Goering. He is a 'bourgeois' with all the outer aspect of respectability, all the habits of a good *paterfamilias* who does not betray his wife and anxiously seeks to secure a future for his children, and he has consciously built up his newest terror organization, covering the whole country, on the assumption that most people are not Bohemians nor fanatics, nor adventurers, nor sex maniacs, nor sadists, but first and foremost jobholders, and good family men.

"It was *Péguy*, I believe, who *called the family man the 'grand aventurier du 20e siècle.'* He died too soon to learn that he was also the great criminal of the century. We had been so accustomed to admire or gently ridicule the family man's kind concern and earnest concentration on the welfare of his family, his solemn determination to make life easy for his wife and children, that we hardly noticed how the devoted *paterfamilias*, worried about nothing so much as his security, was transformed under the pressure of the chaotic economic conditions of our time into an involuntary adventurer, who for all his industry and care could never be certain what the next day would bring. The docility of this type was already manifest in the very early period of Nazi 'Gleichschaltung.' It became clear that for the sake of his pension, his life insurance, the security of his wife and children, such a man was ready to sacrifice his beliefs, his honor, his human dignity. It needed only the Satanic genius of Himmler to discover that after such degradation he was entirely prepared to do literally anything when the ante was raised and the bare existence of his family threatened. The only condition he put was that he should be fully exempted from responsibility for his acts. Thus that very person, the average German, whom the Nazis notwithstanding years of the most furious propaganda could not induce to kill a Jew on his own account . . . , now serves the machine of destruction without opposition. In contrast to the earlier units of the SS men and Gestapo, Himmler's over-all organization relies not on fanatics, nor on congenital murderers, nor on sadists, it relies entirely upon the normality of jobholders and family men.[3]

---

3. In the German version from which Blumenberg quotes here, this sentence concludes: ". . . it relies entirely upon men of Heinrich Himmler's sort." (Trans.)

"... It requires no particular national character to supply this new type of functionary.... It is not even certain that they would do the work if it were only their own lives and future that were at stake. They felt (after they no longer needed to fear God, their conscience cleared through the bureaucratic organization of their acts) only the responsibility toward their own families. *The transformation of the family man* from a responsible member of society, interested in all public affairs, to a 'bourgeois' concerned only with his private existence and knowing no civic virtue, is an international modern phenomenon. The exigencies of our time ... can at any moment transform him into the mob man and make him the instrument of whatsoever madness and horror. Each time society, through unemployment, frustrates the small man in his normal functioning and normal self-respect, it trains him for that last stage in which he will willingly undertake any function, even that of hangman.... It is true that the development of this modern type of man, who is the exact opposite of the 'citoyen' and whom for lack of a better name we have called the 'bourgeois,' enjoyed particularly favorable conditions in Germany. Hardly another country of Occidental culture was so little imbued with the classic virtues of civic behavior. In no other country did private life and private calculations play so great a role. ... What we have called the 'bourgeois' [*der Spießer*] is the modern man of the masses, not in his exalted moments of collective excitement, but in the security (today one should say the insecurity) of his own private domain."

The Symbol of the Pariah: The Problem of the Murderous Family Men[4]

How was it possible that in the past epoch, it was not the dangerous habitual criminal, the antisocial outsider, who was roped into the organization of murder and made the executor of its actions, but the "respectable" citizen, the "family man"? Hannah Arendt

---

4. Review of *Sechs Essays* (Heidelberg: Lambert Schneider, 1948), the first book published by Hannah Arendt in Germany after 1945, printed in the newspaper *Die Welt* on 16 November 1948. Blumenberg signed "Bb." A revised edition of *Sechs Essays* was published as *Die verborgene Tradition* (Frankfurt: Suhrkamp, 1976). [There is no direct English equivalent. (Trans.)]

tries to answer this question in one of her *Six Essays*, recently published by Lambert Schneider, Heidelberg. She develops her explanation for this stupefying paradox from the phenomenon of the pariah, which experiences a modern revival, in a totalitarian system, precisely in the *Spießbürger*[5] and *paterfamilias*. He in particular is driven by the constant threat to his elementary existence and bare being—not just his own, but also his family's—to desperate obedience, to abandon morality, and to disregard guilt; it drives him into the situation of the pariah, who has but one choice left: to be a useful object or not to be at all. And even to make this decision the modern pariah, whom "Organized Guilt" (the essay's title) reduced to a tiny particle of its organization, lacks the human substance.

How was it possible, Hannah Arendt goes on to ask in an essay "On Imperialism,"[6] that a handful of men could drag entire nations into a bloody frenzy? Here too the symbol of the pariah provides a key and an answer. The creation of the "mob," that underclass to whom the goods and rights of life are denied, which has nothing to lose and can thus be won over to vague causes and ruthless means, is the precondition for imperialism and its bloody games.

A mere twenty years ago, the pariah was, to us, a phenomenon specific to Asian countries. No longer to recognize the human in an outcast group of humans seemed alien to European thought. Yet these essays testify to the fact that, for a long time and in shifting forms, pariahdom has been part of modern lived reality. They connect the experience of the Jewish pariahdom of our times with the urgency of the philosophical viewpoint that the author acquired in the school of Karl Jaspers.

What thus emerges here, besides a discussion of the contemporary philosophy of existentialism, is the hidden tradition of the Jewish people in some of their exemplary figures. From Heine to Franz

---

5. Not merely a "respectable citizen," but something of a "little man" with aggressive tendencies and culturally a "philistine." (Trans.)

6. No English version of this essay appears to have been published; its argument is related to that of *The Origins of Totalitarianism*. (Trans.)

Kafka, we see how the lot of pariahdom is suffered, the powerless claim to a home (*Heimat*), the misery of the pariah, who "hopes yet to become a parvenu." Here is prefigured the fate toward which man is today drifting.

Another essay is given over to representing the work of Franz Kafka as the great symbolism of the pariah. Never before has the fate in which Kafka's characters ultimately originate been so clearly felt and expressed. Kafka's man, suffering from an ineffable guilt, who, thirsting to feel at home somewhere, finally succumbs powerless and exhausted to immense forces—this man, the ultimate pariah, is the one in which today's generation recognizes itself.

[Some States Are Founded by Their Enemies][7]

Some states are founded by their enemies. Nobody else could have managed to confront the improbability of their existence. They exist, although or because everything that might otherwise have favored their establishment was too weak, too benign, too ideal, too literary to prevail against a world of opposition. But then: there they are, because nobody wanted them except those who had finally destroyed the conditions of their possibility. The nicest recognition they stand to gain is a reputation for having paid all their debts. In the last century, since France paid the full contribution of 1871 to the Prussian war chest in the Juliusturm,[8] only Finland has achieved this twice—this country that would be impossible but for its only perpetual enemy.

Was It Permissible to Trivialize Eichmann as a Clown?[9]

When Hannah Arendt published *Eichmann in Jerusalem* in 1964 and wrote that Eichmann impressed her as a clown, this claim was not a piece of irony, but of monstrous cynicism. Hannah Arendt had

---

7. Index card, date impossible to establish, card file 26; title added by the editor.
8. A tower of the Spandau Citadel where a portion of the gold coin extracted from France as reparation after the Franco-Prussian War was stored. (Trans.)
9. Index card 16967 [1976], ESCHAT [Eschatologie], card file 26.

completely failed to recognize the cathartic significance of the official[10] act of getting the man guilty of genocide out of his South American hideout and bringing him to justice amid the country and the people whose doom and statehood this man had both caused, in one case without intending to do so. He was the secret founding figure of this state, on whom must be performed the cleansing act that was both a great revenge and a mythical perpetuation, in order to deal with the past or to save, to win, the past for itself. Sigmund Freud should have written the book, he would have understood the dimension. Hannah Arendt, as she told her German interviewer Gaus on TV, never understood, which is why she was reprimanded, accused of lacking in love for the Jews—she would have been suspicious of such love, for she herself . . . No, then she just ought not to have written this book of incomprehension—she should have been reprimanded not for how she wrote, but for having written at all, she should have reprimanded herself. Incomprehension of a mythical necessity of archaic violence— of the same kind that drove Christians to persecute the murderers of their God's son for millennia. Here, the persecuted did something adequate, and one must simply see that they did it for their historical hygiene. Adolf Eichmann may have been a perpetrator, but who could be the perpetrator of a crime that resulted from a monstrous intellectual defamation, in so anonymous a manner all and none were guilty. But that is unbearable, as unbearable as the idea that no one should be guilty for the rotten state of the world, the very unbearableness that produced anti-Semitism, which itself is just a myth. The captured malefactor can impossibly have been a clown; that is a slight upon his victims, who had hastily submitted to him—here too, not the murderer, but the murdered is guilty: he took the buffoonery seriously, rather than rendering it impossible with laughter.

The Enemy as the State's Founder Cannot Be a Clown[11]

This theorist of politics, who in 1964 thanks her interviewer Gaus for not addressing her as a philosopher, because she considers

---

10. *staatlich*; transcription uncertain.
11. Index card 18417 [1977], POL [Politik], card file 26.

herself a political scientist or some other piece [. . .],¹² is completely insensitive to the political. Confronted with some things from her *Eichmann in Jerusalem*, she keeps thinking that it is a lack of piety toward the victims that she is being accused of—besides the untenable charge of having declared the victims guilty of murder. But the book's decisive political affront is the failure to recognize the public function of Eichmann's capture and execution—the only one ever to have taken place in Israel. This is a matter not of the victims' descendants, but of the people of a state to have caught and judged its historic enemy, as it would have been of the Germans if they could have had their Nuremberg. And that is why it should never have been said that this man had ultimately been a clown (as in A. Reif, *Gespräche mit Hannah Arendt*, 26¹³)—for to capture and judge a clown is a distastrous act of state, the greatest act of state beside that state's great contemporary wars, indeed superior to them. This man must not be accorded the harmlessness of an insignificant cause of terrible events. Hitler can be undemonized because the Germans failed to bring him to justice; Eichmann, judged in the heart of a state that would not have emerged without him, cannot stand before that court as a clown—that can only have been a phenotype, the self-desubstantiating phantom of a figure that could only "make" history once it had been brought to justice.

What Myth Is to Be Told?¹⁴

What Hannah Arendt does not understand about the whole Eichmann trial is the veiled tendency to provide the Israeli state with a founding myth. For that reason too the crime had to be directed with most monstrous exclusivity against the Jewish people and not be "internationalized" as a crime against humanity.

---

12. Illegible, perhaps "für sonst ein Stück vom Weltgeist."
13. Adelbert Reif, ed., *Gespräche mit Hannah Arendt* (Munich, 1976), 26. See p. 27, n. 97 on "Moses the Egyptian."
14. Index card 19101 [1978], JDT [Judentum], "Eichmann in Jerusalem," card file 26.

But also precisely not internalized as personal legal culpability with a feeling of guilt—for Eichmann evidently lacked any such thing. The monster's conscience is clear, he is killed, not punished, made to disappear from the Earth (the ashes sprinkled not on the Holy Land, but at sea). It is "long-forgotten propositions" that are guiding the process here, including those of *ius talionis*, even revenge. The paradox is: he, without whom the state would likely not have been founded, becomes its only lawfully executed victim. Hannah Arendt makes her myth (*EJ*, 278–279)[15] applicable to all humanity because she does not want to leave Zionism its figure of reference: because Eichmann had appointed himself judge over who was and who was not permitted to inhabit the Earth, for Arendt nobody could be expected to share the earth with such a person (and his claim). But precisely that would have removed him from his function of entering the national myth as the vanquished enemy.

Zionism Compromised[16]

Not only Eichmann is a buffoon. Much worse is the fact that Hannah Arendt gives the victims themselves a share in the blame for their doom. Historically justified, but from the distance of one who does not know what it means to want to save one's skin, even without the "immediate threat" of one's own destruction. What does imminent mean, anyway? And is "immediate" not far easier to bear courageously than mediate?

Does Hannah Arendt really believe that without the help of the elders and the councils the whole thing would not have worked? She accuses those who thought that something could be salvaged or who merely pretended to know reality, a reality of the incredible,

---

15. The page references here and in the following texts were inserted by Blumenberg himself, referring to the first German edition. They have been replaced with the corresponding page numbers in the English edition wherever possible. The editor notes that no copy of *Eichmann in Jerusalem* is to be found among those books of Blumenberg's preserved at Marbach. (Trans.)

16. Index card 19102 [1978], JDT, "Eichmann in Jerusalem," card file 26.

which nobody can be expected to reckon with. But Hannah Arendt demands also to think the incredible, namely, the possibility of resistance to a machine with which the world was unable to deal. The whole thing would just not have occurred so discretely, would have had to stack the bodies in old salt mines, for instance. But it would have worked, Hannah Arendt doesn't know what else would.

The stereotypical question, why did one not rebel,[17] served only as smoke screen against the more important question, why did one participate—the victims themselves, not rebelling, are to be incriminated instead of the functionaries, who participated and who Hannah Arendt does not doubt were Zionists. Those who resisted were others, with whom the Zionists could not at any rate identify unreservedly. The American emigrant does not want the founders of the State of Israel to have a monopoly on heroism. Self-organization prevented, according to Hannah Arendt, *EJ*, 125, that a greater part could have been saved?

Whoever accepts exceptions or even benefits from them strengthens the admissibility of the rule from which he seeks exemption: *EJ*, 132–133. To have spared the notables was immoral, the Germans still regretted the expulsion of Einstein, not that of little Hans C.[18] (*EJ*, 134), that's nonsense: that which is at hand takes the place of the ineffable, to lay a hand on Einstein paved the way to killing the nameless!

Not even Eichmann lies to the Hungarian Zionists, while he plays the protector in front of the others (*EJ*, 198–199).

[Handwritten addition:] Because all the judges were Zionists, Eichmann could not make the claim against them that they had different premises for the Jewish question than he (*EJ*, 208–209!). The judges' complicity in this tendency (*EJ*, 209).

---

17. *EJ*, 124; cf. *EJG*, 12.
18. Arendt writes "little Hans Cohn."

### A Belated Founding Act[19]

Hannah Arendt uses categories of the theatrical, the show trial liberally, because Ben Gurion intended to give the trial a function other than the juridical: that of a monument to the founding act, Israel's founding legitimacy. A historic scene was not reenacted [*nachgespielt*], but performed belatedly [*nachgeholt*]: the resistance put up by the Jews against their destroyers, instead of the placeholder war against the Arabs, the symbolic killing of an enemy—not a defendant—was set in motion, justified. Hannah Arendt sees all this juridically, because she does not want to know a state of exception and, as a US citizen, cannot know it. The Federal Republic would have been able neither to pass the death sentence nor to kill Eichmann as its enemy. Of course this is not the judges' intention, but the function of the arrest and trial—Hannah Arendt makes no distinction. Naturally, it is the prosecution, bound by [political] instructions, that Hannah Arendt mocks, that she scornfully finds incompetent to prove what it had announced it would prove, although, had it succeeded in doing so, it would precisely not have fallen under the "one" special law: *EJ*, 22.

The worst thing was probably that the prosecuting counsel, after the execution, made public that the psychiatric reports had described Eichmann as a sadistic and murderous personality, a circumstance that would have precluded punishment (*EJ*, 26)—but precisely not putting him to death! The execution was to be made legal, not the legitimacy of the killing claimed! (Bb)[20] This intelligence of the smallest dimensions would never have come up with the idea of the "final solution": *EJ*, 31. That suits Hannah Arendt and her concept of the petit bourgeois run wild—but can it suit the concept of a state's negative founding figure? That an Eichmann, a functionary, if not a demon of anti-Semitism, should come about because he was "bored to distraction" (*EJ*, 35), and thus by a remove the State of Israel, is more than the reader can bear

---

19. Index card 19103 [1978], JDT, "Eichmann in Jerusalem," card file 26.
20. Abbreviation for Blumenberg.

(+*EJ*, 37). The comedy of the horrific in Eichmann's mouth (*EJ*, 48–49), a kind of Jürgen von Manger effect![21] (Bb) from Solingen, no less. +*EJ*, 50: comedy. "clown" first *EJ*, 54.

Must one tell the truth? Perhaps. Must one always tell the truth? Surely not. Had one to tell the truth at that moment? that this negative founder of the state was a buffoon? He is the one who is always late and made [to look] incompetent, so not the giant demon, who indirectly forces the founding of a state (*EJ*, 82).

The formula: "Build up Eichmann at all costs" (*EJ*, 168).

## The Zionists Begrudged the Negative Superman[22]

The author's keen procedural perception has no sense of the urge of the survivors in the country (20 percent of the population), already called witnesses to the suffering of the Jewish people by the court, to have a voice in a trial onto whose defendant they projected all the atrocities inflicted upon them, often not according to the facts of the matter, but hence "unrightfully"? Whoever can rely upon the last judgment of the court in the Valley of Jehoshaphat, where judgment may also be passed on what someone might have done, had his ubiquity not—as Eichmann's was—been limited, may dispense with taking seriously the imaginary witnesses, who saw Eichmann where he never was (*EJ*, 207). And the judges acted righty in excluding such [testimony] according to procedural norms, not to consider it in sentencing. Yet the author is wrong to treat this as a quantité négligeable for an intellectual. Legally, to the keen Jewish[23] mind, there is no such thing as the singular case, and there must not be. But it just happens to be a unique historical event that the murderer of a people, the organizer of a genocide, thus became the founder of a state and must be killed in some kind of act of state, as the biblical scapegoat was killed for the sins of others,

---

21. Jürgen von Manger: actor and political comic who used the dialect of the Ruhr area as a stylistic device; Eichmann was born in the town of Solingen.
22. Index card 19104 [1978], JDT, "Eichmann in Jerusalem," card file 26.
23. Transcription uncertain.

this one here *also* only for the sins of others, and this is the point Hannah Arendt seeks to make, for those of all Germans. Hannah Arendt is already in a position to criticize the anticipation of the sentence in the arrest in Argentina because her point is not to let Eichmann stand as the sole principal culprit—what then about the culprits who were so insufficiently pursued and punished in Germany, and whose scandalously favorable treatment in contrast to Eichmann is to be underscored? It is a book [arguing] against Eichmann's sole guilt and for the responsibility of the Germans, at least insofar as their lag in atoning [for their crimes] is concerned. I do not disapprove of this tendency, but it comes at the expense of Eichmann's singular role for the Jewish state and his roots in Zionism + Eichmann!!

Hannah Arendt begrudges the Zionists their negative superman. Instead she wishes to postulate a people of negative supermen, the Germans, who brought forth this breed of murderous bureaucrats, did not resist like the Danes, and especially went on to play down what they were involved in. If strict legality had prevailed, the judges would have had to dismiss Hausner's indictment, without changing anything about the outcome: *EJ*, 219, but then Eichmann would have been a different culprit, an accessory to murder, not a negative superman.

Zionism Taken at Its Word[24]

And there is another serious matter: Hannah Arendt indirectly accuses Zionism, for which she has no time, of having infected Eichmann with the idea of the expulsion (not the extermination) of European Jewry. He took them at their word by remolding the formula about giving them "some firm ground under their feet"[25] into that of their own soil, their own country (e.g., *EJ*, 56), and when he was no longer able to evacuate them (because of the war), extermination was to him a remolding of the idea of expulsion. Hence the

---

24. Index card 19105 [1978], JDT, "Eichmann in Jerusalem," card file 26.
25. *EJ*, 103.

emphasis on Eichmann's entire knowledge of Judaism stemming from Herzl's *Judenstaat*, surely not the untruth, but a truth simply unbearable for the present generation—he had only taken that state's ideologue quite exactly at his word!

Eichmann's behavior toward the Jewish emissaries from Palestine, his invitation there, may to Hannah Arendt, the intellectual, be little more than a farce [*Schelmenstück*] (*EJ*, 60–63), but to the Israeli state myth it is a shameful cautionary tale [*Lehrstück*].

The Nazis had encouraged Zionism (*EJ*, 75), imitated it in the Radom State[26]—what odium! And again in the *Reichsprotektorat*: *EJ*, 80.[27]

Better [to Have] Equality in Doom?[28]

Not only did Sergeant Anton Schmidt[29] give help, he also did something unprecedented in this whole story: "He did not do it for money"! (Arendt, *EJ*, 230).[30] Of course it's great that he didn't take any money. On the other hand, all this also belongs in a story entitled "Money must be able to buy anything!" For if there were any lacunae at all in the apparatus of total destruction, they were caused by money, although of course money was also taken with nothing given in return. But is not precisely that the despicable thing, that rich people could buy their freedom? Counter-question: would it have been better if, for reasons of justice and equality, they too had perished? The whole problem with the notables: would it have been better, had these *Verdienstjuden*[31] etc. not existed? Israel would have come into being, but it would have lacked

---

26. In Jerusalem, Eichmann mentioned the plan to create a "Jewish state" around Radom; the actual deportation ("resettlement") of Jews to the Lublin District (*Nisko-Projekt*) began in October 1939.

27. I.e., the establishment of the Theresienstadt ghetto in the "Protectorate of Bohemia and Moravia."

28. Index card 19106 [1978], JDT, "Eichmann in Jerusalem," card file 26.

29. See *EJ*, 230.

30. Blumenberg's own reference, originally to *EJG*, 275.

31. Jews given preferential treatment for reasons such as prior military service. (Trans.)

people whose eminence was perhaps not in every case groundless. But even supposing that the exceptions had been completely unjustified—would it have been better, following Hannah Arendt's moralism, if they too had been murdered?

### Last Words of the Negative State Founder[32]

Adolf Eichmann was the only person in the legal history of the State of Israel to be sentenced to death and executed. His ashes were scattered over the Mediterranean Sea: a last act of *diaspora* in the literal sense.

Before his execution, he had said to his judges: "After a short while, gentlemen, *we shall all meet again*. Such is the fate of all men. I was a *Gottgläubiger* in life, and a *Gottgläubiger* I die."[33]

These words have been subsumed under that "banality of evil" with which Hannah Arendt had sought to grasp the phenomenon of the misdeeds of the Hitler regime. But was this not rather the malice [*die Bosheit*] of banality?

There were no articles of faith for *Gottgläubige*. Their Germanism, however, seemed to oblige them to expect and promote their afterlife not in their individual identity, but in their tribe. In [the form of] his descendants, everyone could make provision for not vanishing into nothingness. Genetic identity, thought strictly enough, formed the biologistic meaning of this idea of immortality. It was more than the metaphor of mere continuity of a line of descent.

At some point, Adolf Eichmann must have formed an idea of all this for himself that ran counter to his order's code.[34] He would

---

32. Undated typescript, UNF 2398–2399.
33. *EJ*, 252. The last sentence is not in the English version, and is translated here straight from the German. In the English version, Arendt explains the term *Gottgläubiger* as follows, without quoting Eichmann directly: "He began by stating emphatically that he was a *Gottgläubiger*, to express in common Nazi fashion that he was no Christian and did not believe in life after death." The German version (*EJG*, 300) draws attention to the contradiction between the two parts of Eichmann's statement. (Trans.)
34. His order: i.e., the SS. (Trans.)

survive his death and meet again those who had brought it about. Those who had to listen to these last words must have been chilled to the bone to hear someone not only threatening to encounter them in the hereafter, but to continue to live with them on an equal footing—on the same 'ground' of that unknown land from which no wanderer ever returns.

What monstrosity lay in Eichmann's valediction[35] can perhaps be made clearer by the imaginary address of the judges with which Hannah Arendt concludes her controversial book on Eichmann, in order to put in place of the 'subjective sense of injustice' the undeniable satisfaction of the desire, by exacting the ultimate penalty, no longer to keep on living with one who had arrogated to himself "to determine who should and who should not inhabit the world."[36] But "no member of the human race [could] be expected to share the earth with those who desire and enact such things."[37] And she concludes her fictional judgment of 1963 and her whole book with the sentence "This is the reason, and the only reason, you must hang."[38]

Adolf Eichmann cannot have known of this turn against the whole trial and its sensitivities in framing his last words. But he utters them as if to spite Hannah Arendt's last words on his case. It was this very 'commonality' beyond the grave, awaiting both him and his judges, that constituted his threat.

To give an idea of how far his monstrous logic went, the comparison with the fictional judgment of the rigorist Hannah Arendt may quite suffice. One had the murderer of a people, the man who kept the minutes at the Wannsee Conference, the organizer of what

---

35. *Wiedersehenszuruf*, i.e., a valediction looking ahead to a future encounter. (Trans.)

36. *EJ*, 279. (Trans.)

37. Ibid.; again, the quotation from the English version has been amended to take account of the German text from which Blumenberg quotes (*EJG*, 329). (Trans.)

38. *EJ*, 279. These are indeed the last words of the first German edition, which lacks the postscript appended to the currently available editions in English and German. (Trans.)

was nearly impossible to carry out, tried and sentenced to lay down all he had according to the *ius talionis*: his life. But it was for this that he claimed, once he had made amends, to be equal with his judges.

He was also one to stay on his bond.[39] He could die only one death for the millions of deaths to which he had lent his hand. And before he died it, he appealed to a casuistry that he might have learned from the rabbis and from Saint Paul's Epistle to the Romans when he was busy preparing for his 'vocation.' He invoked the legal premise of 'justification': he who dies the death, has the acquittal.[40]

A *gottgläubig* Talmudist—that was quite a *tremendum* as the last word of the head of the Department of Jewish Affairs at the Reich Main Security Office [*Reichssicherheitshauptamt*].

---

39. *Auch war er einer, der auf seinem Schein bestand*, a reference to *The Merchant of Venice* (4.1), in which Shylock, insisting in court on his pound of flesh, proclaims: "I stay here on my bond." (Trans.)

40. Romans 6:7: "For he that is dead is freed from sin."

# III

# THEMATICALLY RELATED TEXTS FROM THE NACHLASS

### The Power of Truth[1]

Among the intimate convictions of European history is that the truth will triumph.

That is as little self-evident as can be, considering what measure of description and polemic was deployed in order to represent and warn against rhetorical distractions up to the possibilities of demagogy.

The gods, too, were after all in alliance with the truth from the beginning. They had no investment in man's knowledge. The means of their power was not truth, but cunning.

Only a god who seemed to think it important that human beings learned the truth about the world and themselves could be seen as

---

1. Undated typescript, UNF 574–575a.

an ally of truth and could give it the prospect of an ultimate victory, albeit in the form of an otherworldly intuition.²

Now one might say that an estimate of the truth's chances of prevailing is a matter of estimating humans and their reason—or also of that which stands against their reason. One may then come to the result that, ultimately, untruth triumphed in the world no differently than malice. After all, science too was in each of its phases nothing but its state-of-the-art errors.

But there is an even more ingenious way of combining the two basic claims about science, that of its constitutive victories and that of its inevitable defeats, that of its power and that of its powerlessness. This is to make of objection and resistance to a truth an indication of the truthfulness of that very truth. Only the overcoming of this resistance finally brings the doubters to the fore, if the most important of indications were no longer to be trusted.

Freud and his school not only expected resistance—that of their patients, their professional colleagues, the world at large, both science and the public—and factored it into their prognostications of [their] fate, but practically declared it to be that necessity whose absence would have marked psychoanalysis with the stamp of error.

In order to do so, it was of course necessary to subject the phenomena of resistance to a finely calibrated measurement procedure. When, in Freud's school, concern grew that analysis, because of the investment in time involved, could be available only to the pecuniary means of few, and one began to advocate certain methods of abbreviation, acceleration, and grouping, Freud saw in this activity of the school's 'therapeutic wing' the final and most threatening form of resistance. And this at a moment in which all the world was already making a point of discussing its sexual problems in cafés using the language of psychoanalysis. The diminution of

---

2. *In Gestalt einer allerdings erst jenseitigen Anschauung*; see above, p. 22, n. 72. (Trans.)

resistance was more threatening than the emergence of its final and once more intensified, because it was professional and [emerged from] within the school, form.

The general premise for resistance as a criterion might be [this]: what people gladly accept cannot be the truth. The condition for this, in turn, is that people are constituted in such a way as not to accept the truth, because it imposes upon their nature—impositions of a kind that would bring about a definitive but unwelcome improvement of the latter.

But however indispensable resistance is according to this para-theory, however heroic standing firm against it may make one look—one is tempted to say: resistance to resistance, as certain is that what is *behind* this desirability of high risks in trying out the new is the all-bearing or all-framing conviction that resistance taken as a whole will not at any rate be fatal to the cause.

Why ever not? Why should none of these forms of resistance ultimately do away with a scientific theory? Freud, threatened all around by dangers, never believed in this. This trait allows [one] to comprehend that for him, too, the conviction of the indispensability of resistance was in turn undergirded with the conviction of the power of truth, its survival, its growing stronger even in the face of resistance.

The facts of the matter have grown more complicated. In principle, it seems to have remained indispensable that alliances between history and truth belong to our standard of appraising both.

## Anti-Semitism and Jewish Self-Abnegation[3]

It has often been seen how the particular historical and social situation of Jewry has driven the Jew to an anarchic opposition, a

---

3. Index card 860, Judenfrage, card file 23; dated by Blumenberg to "July 1947."

destructive *ressentiment* against the historically developed[4] social order. It has been less remarked upon that this attitude is only one of the realized possibilities of his situation. The fascination of phenomena, from participation in which he is excluded, a wistful admiration, indeed adoration, is another Jewish possibility. Its most significant representative is Walther Rathenau. He glorified the Germanic race, the Siegfried type, and in doing so laid [part of the] ground for its terrible apotheoses. He lovingly surrendered to the phenomenon of the Prussian aristocracy and for its benefit devised the schema of "people of courage" and "people of fear."[5] All that the Jewish mind, his own, still represents to him is a sublimation of fear, for the Jews are the ultimate people of fear. Here, the phenomenon of anti-Semitism is traced back to its most secret and dangerous root. It is this unique "schizophrenia" that, from the force of longing to be itself no more, cleaves the Jewish consciousness. Not only in the intensity with which he made his affective claim, but more still in the ideological grounding, did Rathenau leave Treitschke and Lagarde behind him in their anti-Semitism—according to a remark by Maximilian Harden.[6] The anti-Semitism of the strangers is preceded by the self-abnegation and cloven consciousness of Jewry.

---

4. Because *geschichtlich* may be understood both as an adverb and as an adjective in this context, *geschichtlich geworden* might mean "become historic" as well as "historically developed." (Trans.)

5. *Mutmenschen* and *Furchtmenschen*. (Trans.)

6. Maximilian Harden (1861–1927), German Jewish writer (converted to Protestantism), known for his central role in the Eulenburg affair over allegations of homosexuality in Kaiser Wilhelm II's entourage. The comment to which Blumenberg refers here may be one Harden made to accompany the republication, in 1922, of Rathenau's famous prewar essay, "Höre, Israel!" Harden accuses Rathenau of surpassing the notorious anti-Semites Heinrich von Treitschke, Paul de Lagarde, and Richard Wagner in demanding that Jews effectively cease to be Jewish and postulating Germanization as their highest aim. See Maximilian Harden, "In der Mördergrube," *Die Zukunft*, vol. 118, July 1, 1922, 11–12; quoted in Sabine Armbrecht, *Verkannte Liebe: Maximilian Hardens Haltung zu Deutschtum und Judentum* (Oldenburg: Bis, 1999), 164; online at http://oops.uni-oldenburg.de/582/1/615.pdf. (Trans.)

## [Ambiguity without Comprehension][7]

Thomas Mann is, at the height of the Second World War, barely a month after Hitler's attack on Russia, invited to a housewarming party[8] at the Horkheimers', which mushrooms into a *historical-political-philosophical conversation orgy of a fairly tortuous variety*. We learn what may have tormented the writer working on the final volume of "Joseph" from a single sentence in the diary for 12 July 1941: *These Jews have a sense of Hitler's greatness that I cannot bear.*

This note does not deserve to be passed over with a shrug. It touches a deep spot of the phenomenon of enmity. Thomas Mann was certainly an active enemy of Hitler, driven by a loathing of the figure's inhumanity, which to him consisted of history making as adventuring. Nonetheless Thomas Mann was not a genuine enemy of Hitler. One may put this to the test by imagining Hitler as an early reader of the "Reflections of a Non-Political Man" of 1918—if we knew of such a thing, many a desire for explanation would be fulfilled. To imagine Thomas Mann in the representative role of the Reich poet à la Gerhart Hauptmann, under the particular and personal protection of the con man Hermann Göring—that's not altogether inconceivable. Hitler is not his enemy of old. This enmity has something of apostasy about it and of the need to prove oneself, of the overeagerness of the convert who is keeping watch over the others [to make sure] that they too are good enemies.

So here he is bothered by these Jews, who are unable to find small the man who is all set to be the doom of their people. This will be repeated two decades later in Jerusalem, when Hannah Arendt will see in Adolf Eichmann, brought to justice before the people that was his victim, a buffoon of pathetic insignificance: she is surprised at the dismay this causes.

---

7. Undated typescript [ca. 1982], collection "Textsammlung zu Thomas Mann"; title added by archivist at DLA Marbach.
8. In English: "Housewarmingparty." (Trans.)

Thomas Mann anticipates this ambiguity without comprehension. It means little to him that he was going to survive this Hitler, or would have done, if he had remained in the country. He would have been shaken by revulsion, but he would have availed himself of the subtleties of contempt of which he was capable and of which others availed themselves. He would have found Hitler pathetic and hated him as one not worth the historic effort it took to destroy him. All that did not exist for those whose sense of Hitler's greatness Thomas Mann in faraway California could not bear: their enemy, in his apocalyptic uniqueness, had to fill the historic dimension in which he emerged. For he fulfilled a destiny, which these open or disguised Hegelians could after all see only under the rubric of the 'cunning of reason.' No, he too, to whom this was unbearable, was right.

## [Hated for Millennia][9]

It stands to reason that, after the genocide that Hitler had prepared for the Jews, the efforts of thought it took to discover the secret of such hatred had to be immense.

It seems to me that analytical profundity can easily tempt [one] to discount a drastic 'superficiality' in the syndrome of the hatred of this little people, which spans time and the world. Artificial profundities give the matter a dignity that should be accorded those killed, not the murderer. Also not those who would see upon a banal disgruntlement, a random antipathy bestowed the succor of a quasi-metaphysical demonism, if they still set any store by

---

9. Undated typescript [ca. 1980], UNF 2448; title added by archivist at DLA Marbach; source for the quotations in italics given on the reverse: "Erwin Blumenfeld, Durch tausendjährige Zeit. Erinnerungen. Frauenfeld 1976, München 1980, 51." The German Jewish photographer Erwin Blumenfeld emigrated to the United States via France in 1941; his autobiography, to which Blumenberg refers here, was published as a paperback in 1980 and was reprinted several times and appeared in English as *Eye to I: The Autobiography of a Photographer* (New York: Thames and Hudson, 1999).

it. Psychoanalysis provides its clients with a quality they secretly desire: permission to find themselves interesting. This is a favor that the Jew-baiter's analyst all too readily posthumously does his 'object.'

Unfortunately, there is no story to tell, as Freud for instance tried, that might explain something. Was Pilate perhaps less guilty of Jesus's death than the high priests? Peter more harmless than Caiphas? Does Bach's St. Matthew Passion belong to the history of anti-Semitism? No, the blame for Jesus's death, too, was only ever a rhetorical cliché. Then to dispense with explanations?

That, in turn, would only help the aficionados of mere demonology. But there is something trivial about the matter, through which the age of this enmity, in particular, must also be grasped.

I will not say that this was the most apt of all discussions I have read, but it is probably the most plausible connection between surface and depth that one who, on encountering the sign *No dogs! No Jews! No niggers!*[10] in 1943 as an emigrant in Florida, could imagine only *one* source of hatred, which would at the same time have been that of the sense of election: hated for millennia, because this people *could always read and write*.

## Banality as the Root of Evil as Extravagance[11]

Hannah Arendt spoke of the banality of evil as the characteristic trait of totalitarianism, which was capable of turning a plain family man into a murderer. Expressed thus, it looks as though banality were some kind of costume donned by evil, all the easier to creep into the morality of a bourgeois lifestyle.

The decisive question that this fails to ask or indeed omits is whether evil does not, as it were, emerge from banality, is its aberrant flower, or indeed the exit, the means of escape from banality. This must surely apply when bearing in mind the intellectuals'

---

10. In English; originally "jews." (Trans.)
11. Index card, not datable, TERM [Terminologie], Unbehagen, card file 26.

horror of banality; it is what they fear as the always expected and always already familiar way of life, which they too are bound for if they do not take decisive measures against it. These measures almost inevitably take the form of evil, for how else to act against the despised harmlessness of unbearable everyday life than by creating opportunities for the extraordinary, that is to say, that which is disorderly, contrary to order? Opportunities for evil and such forms of testing one's extraordinariness almost always present themselves; this is then downplayed by a pretense of perspectivism: it was the standpoint of the banal bourgeois himself that disqualified the altogether other as an evil confronting him and seeking to force him beyond the limits of his commonplaceness. This is a repetition, on an incomparably more dangerous level, of a process that has many times been tried out in the aesthetic milieu: as the artist's secession from the zone of norms and normality, decried as academic, to the realm of specialness and the liberation from norms, a zone in which one is furthermore compelled constantly to confirm the exception from banality by daring feats of extravagance—for extravagance is a dare that may begin with a harmless way of dressing or undressing and end with the coldbloodedness of unmotivated murder.

## The Shortest German Joke[12]

—Do you know the shortest German joke [*Witz*] ever?
—No.
—Auschwitz.

---

12. Undated typescript [ca. 1989], UNF 3397. Blumenberg's handwritten note on the reverse: "Auschwitz Oświęcim / 21. Criminal Code Amendment Act of 13 June 1985 'Auschwitz-Lüge' § 194 StGB [*Strafgesetzbuch*, German criminal code] / This place-name remains German / 'Joke' on the metalevel, with only the 2. syllable having (semantic) meaning." ["The 2. syllable" refers to -*witz*, a homophone of the German word for joke, *Witz*, a cognate of the English *wit*. (Trans.)]

A crude pun, to be sure, who could fail to hear that. But surely more than that. Who, if this is supposed to be a joke, is going to laugh about it? Placed there so nakedly it is a blasphemy. Should it want to blaspheme the God who cannot escape the blame—or shift it to the freedom of his creature—that he let Auschwitz happen?

But that is not it. One must take into account the tone of voice in which this short dialogue—which surely only looks as though it could have become one—takes place. The question is posed by a Jew, by George Tabori, and it is not framed in such a way that one would have to fight it off: I want to know everything but the shortest German joke. A trap, then. For the asker knows what he will wreak: an awkwardness that no Socrates could have imagined. Accordingly, it must be added, there follows no answer from Herlinde Koelbl to the man of the theater's punch line.[13]

What must not be ignored: the Jew Tabori, who has already told profound Jewish jokes in interviews, announces a German joke and moreover one that he can never have heard from a German. It is a German joke from the school of the objective spirit. This is why one cannot tell it to others: precautions are not enough to shield oneself in doing so. A Jew has let himself think up the shortest German joke—and if one considers it thus, one can even understand that it didn't cost him much effort. For tragedy and comedy converge in the absolute crime: the tragedy of the victims, the comedy of the perpetrators, whose statures stand in no relation to what they have wrought. It is the comedy that Hannah Arendt did not grasp when she saw the little wretch[14] Eichmann shrink in

---

13. Herlinde Koelbl, *Jüdische Portraits: Photographien und Interviews* (Frankfurt: Fischer, 1989), 238.
14. *Würstchen*, likely a play on *Hanswurst*, the term used in the German edition of *Eichmann in Jerusalem* for "clown." (Trans.)

the glass cage of the dock in Jerusalem, because she could or would not recognize that this was the negative hero of the State of Israel, its founder not even altogether against his will. After all, he did once think about Madagascar.

The Jew Tabori dares to tell a German joke. But who laughs about it? It is laughter postponed. It assumes that the topsy-turvy world of the perpetrators' success has burnished the aura of a Jewry already vanishing into assimilation—will have burnished it even if the whole world's censure should be concentrated on discriminating against the means of that state's self-assertion. It is a German joke if nuclear missiles grow in the bunkers beneath the Negev, with which the survivors *could* pay back their parents' murderers according to the *ius talionis*. In the potential of what the genocide for all its bureaucratic-technical perfection failed to accomplish, as a free-floating option, lies the German joke, which remains a joke by excluding its own assumptions.

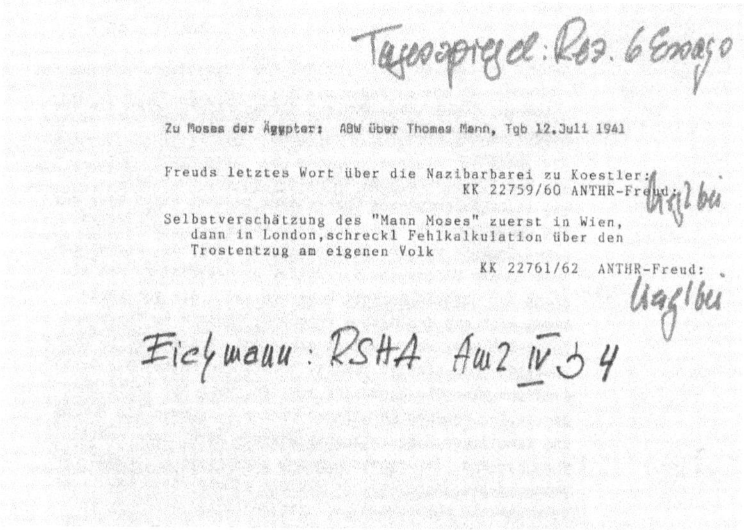

*Tagesspiegel: Rez. 6 Enxago*

```
Zu Moses der Ägypter:   ABW über Thomas Mann, Tgb 12.Juli 1941

Freuds letztes Wort über die Nazibarbarei zu Koestler:
                                    KK 22759/60  ANTHR-Freud: *unglbu*

Selbstverschätzung des "Mann Moses" zuerst in Wien,
    dann in London, schreckl Fehlkalkulation über den
    Trostentzug am eigenen Volk
                                    KK 22761/62  ANTHR-Freud: *unglbu*
```

*Eichmann: RSHA Amt IV 3 4*

**Figure 1.** Undated note by Blumenberg: "On Moses the Egyptian."

Hannah Arendt/New York

z . Zt. Koeln, den 3.November 56.

Sehr geehrter Herr Dr. Blumenberg -
ich werde in der naechsten Woche ein paar Tage in Kiel sein und habe Gruesse an Sie von Hans Jonas aus New York, der ein alter guter Freund von mir ist. Es waere schoen, wenn wir uns sprechen koennten. Ich bin ab Dienstag naechster Woche im Park Hotel in Kiel zu erreichen. Vielleicht laeuten Sie mich an, am besten Vormittags.

Mit den besten Empfehlungen,

*Hannah Arendt*

**Figure 2.** Letter from Hannah Arendt to Hans Blumenberg, 3 November 1956.

[Translation]

Hannah Arendt/New York

currently Cologne, 3 November 1956

Dear Dr. Blumenberg,
I shall be spending a few days in Kiel next week and have greetings to you from Hans Jonas in New York, who is an old, good friend of mine. It would be nice if we could talk. I can be reached at the Park Hotel in Kiel from Tuesday next week. Perhaps you can give me a call, preferably in the morning.

With sincerest regards,
Hannah Arendt

Figure 3. The first pages of Blumenberg's 1978 reading log, showing that he began *Eichmann in Jerusalem* on 28 February.

# Editor's Afterword

## I

Since Hans Blumenberg's Nachlass has been made available to scholars, it has been possible to form an image of how the philosopher worked, and on what.[1] In the last decades of his life, he worked mainly on adding to this body of material, writing for himself and perhaps in the hope of furthering a posthumous reputation that by now is truly beyond compare. Since his death in 1996, more books have appeared under his name than he published between 1960 and

---

1. Cf. the editors' informative postscript to Hans Blumenberg, *Quellen, Ströme, Eisberge*, ed. Ulrich von Bülow and Dorit Krusche (Berlin: Suhrkamp, 2012), 271–292, esp. 279–283; and Ulrich von Bülow and Dorit Krusche, "Nachrichten an sich selbst: Der Zettelkasten von Hans Blumenberg," in *Zettelkästen: Maschinen der Phantasie*, ed. Heike Gfrereis and Ellen Strittmatter (Marbach: Deutsche Schillergesellschaft, 2013), 113–119.

1989, and it is doubtful whether they all would have met with his approval. But as his card files, which are now archived, show, Blumenberg directed his efforts from the very beginning toward creating an extensive body of philosophical work that could never be completed. This was matched by the openness of his philosophizing, and while the enterprise as a whole was planned and systematic, more and more incomplete projects accumulated. Whereas Blumenberg had collected 280 index cards over the course of 1945, their number grew to 24,000 by 1984. This vast store of excerpts, comments, and reflections formed Blumenberg's treasury, from which he could compose lecture courses as well as entire books. Any reader wondering why these books often seem to make so many leaps and are full of unexpected connections, why their author largely dispenses with the linear development of his thoughts and with a historical, chronological mode of representation, will learn from researching the Nachlass that Blumenberg's oeuvre is the product not least of the ingenious architecture of his card files.

One might thus be tempted to suspect that it was an idea from the card catalogue, an unexpected juxtaposition, that first brought to light the commonalities between Sigmund Freud and Hannah Arendt, between *Moses and Monotheism* and *Eichmann in Jerusalem*. But that is not the case. The two parts of the essay "Moses the Egyptian," though developed at different stages, are interwoven in the most precise manner. Their critical thrusts are mutually reinforcing. Freud and Arendt are charged with callousness in publishing their respective books. Both had been convinced, it is argued, that a truth, once recognized, must be stated and propagated for the enlightenment of mankind and for its liberation. Blumenberg aptly designates such rigor or "rigorism" as the "absolutism of truth."

However, Blumenberg finds the actual connection between the founder of psychoanalysis and the celebrated political scientist by comparing the implicit effects of their books: "As Freud took Moses the man from his people, so Hannah Arendt took Adolf Eichmann from the State of Israel" (p. 5).[2] Freud's book on

---

2. Parenthetical page references here and below refer to the present edition.

Moses had appeared at the worst moment imaginable in 1939. In trying to prove the Egyptian descent of their founding figure, Freud had knowingly robbed the persecuted Jews of the consolation they drew from their faith and needed in that hour. Blumenberg ascribes a similar effect to Hannah Arendt's controversial report from the Eichmann trial. That Arendt had called the organizer of the Holocaust a "clown" had been an act of monstrous cynicism, a denigration of the State of Israel's negative founding figure. This analogy can be understood only against the background of a defense of myth. For this too is at stake in the unexpected juxtaposition of Freud and Arendt. Blumenberg places myth, be it religious or political, in its human dimension above truth claims of any kind, because myths, unlike the truth, fulfill the human desire for consolation. The figures of the founding prophet and of the conquered enemy are such consoling myths.

Moreover, the essay presented here, taken from the Nachlass and probably not written with publication in mind, contains a biographical substratum. A reason suggests itself for why the philosopher in his later years returned to Freud and Arendt, and why he chose this particular constellation: both represented a specific intellectual attitude toward their own Jewishness, and this will have been what interested Blumenberg and why his own text, as he himself remarked, was marked by such dismay (p. 5).

## II

Blumenberg's closer study of the works of Sigmund Freud began no later than the second half of the 1960s. Freud and his book on Moses[3] are first mentioned in the pathbreaking essay "Wirklichkeitsbegriff und Wirkungspotential des Mythos," which was at the center of the September 1968 conference of the research group Poetik und Hermeneutik, and which inaugurated Blumenberg's

---

3. Blumenberg first read *Moses and Monotheism* in August 1968, after it had appeared in the Bibliothek Suhrkamp series.

examination of problems of the reception of myth, which would continue for over a decade. In that essay, Blumenberg explicitly draws on the model of latency and development, which Freud had developed in his account of neuroses and finally in the "highly controversial speculation on the Egyptian origin of Moses and his religion," in order to illustrate how mythological resources are handed down through the ages.[4] In the expanded edition of the first and second parts of *The Legitimacy of the Modern Age*, "the hypothetical murder of the religion founder in *Moses and Monotheism*" is adduced as an example of the construction of historically unresolved "relations of guilt."[5] In the 1970s and early 1980s, Blumenberg repeatedly applied himself to detailed studies of Freud, as his conscientiously maintained reading logs attest. The fruits of these studies can be found in a lecture course, "Philosophical Elements in Freud," delivered at the University of Münster in the 1980–81 winter semester, as well as in several books,[6] and Freud became one of Blumenberg's "household deities." The index cards under the heading "ANTHR FREUD," which Blumenberg collected as a subset of "Anthropology" and which contain a variety of material used in the Moses essay, can also be dated to between 1975 and 1982.

If one is to understand the development of the fundamental idea that gives the essay its stringency and connects its two parts, it is worth looking at the story of the origins of *Moses and Monotheism*, with which Blumenberg was familiar from the correspondence between Sigmund Freud and Arnold Zweig[7] and which he interpreted in his own way. On a 1982 index card, he summarized

---

4. Blumenberg, "Wirklichkeitsbegriff und Wirkungspotential des Mythos," 19, 24–25, 43. This article also contains the first mention of the phrase "absolutism of truth" (*Absolutismus der Wahrheit*), on 27.

5. Blumenberg, *Legitimacy of the Modern Age*, 117.

6. Blumenberg, *Work on Myth*, 515–522; Blumenberg, *Die Lesbarkeit der Welt* (Frankfurt: Suhrkamp, 1981), 337–371; Blumenberg, *Höhlenausgänge*, 684–699.

7. Blumenberg read this correspondence, which was published in 1968, at the end of 1973, and made several excerpts from it two years later and again in 1982, filing them under "ANTHR FREUD." Already in 1964, he had copied two letters of Freud's referring to the *Moses* book onto index cards; see above, pp. 30–35.

his reading thus: "First overestimation of 'Moses and Monotheism' in Vienna—then underestimation of the consolation denied in London" (above, p. 40). What was by meant by this? Already in the summer of 1933, Freud had told Zweig of his conjecture that Moses—"a strong anti-Semite" who had "made no secret of it"—might have been an Egyptian.[8] A year later, he told Zweig about a work in progress, whose contemporary point of reference was well known to the recipient, a recent emigrant to Palestine: "Faced with the new persecutions"—the National Socialists had just come to power in Germany—one again asked oneself "how the Jews have come to be what they are and why they have attracted this undying hatred. I soon discovered the formula: Moses created the Jews. So I gave my work the title *The Man Moses, a historical novel* [. . .]."[9]

Freud, then, was looking above all for an explanation of the phenomenon of anti-Semitism,[10] and he hoped to find it by going back to the historical beginnings of Judaism. In the third part of the study he intended to reiterate his psychoanalytic theory of religion, which he had first set out in *Totem and Taboo* (1913). But it was precisely this part of the Moses project, dealing with the theory of religion, that for a long time kept him from publishing the

---

8. "Our great master Moses was, after all, a strong anti-Semite and made no secret of it. Perhaps he really was an Egyptian." Freud to Zweig, 18 August 1933, quoted in Max Schur, *Freud: Living and Dying* (New York: International Universities Press, 1972), 468, 563 (Blumenberg noted this passage). An exhaustive appreciation of Freud's interest in the Egypticization of the figure of Moses may be found in Jan Assmann, *Moses the Egyptian: The Memory of Egypt in Western Monotheism* (1998) (Cambridge, MA: Harvard University Press, 2009).

9. Freud to Zweig, 30 September 1934, in *Letters of Sigmund Freud and Arnold Zweig*, 91–92. Blumenberg addressed the question of "how the Jews [. . .] have attracted this undying hatred" in the fragment "Hated for millennia"; see above, p. 62.

10. As late as 1927, Freud had written to Zweig: "With regard to anti-Semitism I don't really want to search for explanations." *Letters of Sigmund Freud and Arnold Zweig*, 3. With regard to Freud's examination of anti-Semitism in terms of his theory of religion, Jan Assmann has made the most important contributions, writing that Freud's "analysis of monotheism and violence is certainly one of the more important contributions of *Moses* to the theory of religion." Assmann, *Moses the Egyptian*, 157.

projected book, because he—in light of the political influence the Catholic Church wielded in Austria—feared a ban on psychoanalysis and the attendant professional disadvantages to his students. Blumenberg considers this an "overestimation" of the possible consequences of *Moses and Monotheism*, one reinforced by Freud identifying his principal enemy in Catholicism while failing to recognize the dangers of National Socialism.

Yet there was another reason why Freud hesitated. In letters to Arnold Zweig, he repeatedly claimed that his work did not "stand up to [his] own criticism," the "weakness" of his "historical construction" keeping him from publishing it.[11] Not until 1937 did Freud decide to publish parts of the manuscript in *Imago*, the Viennese journal he had cofounded, while informing an unnamed correspondent that he had had to withhold "the most important section" of the whole.[12] What was printed were two of the later three parts of *Moses and Monotheism*. The first ("Moses an Egyptian") begins with a famous sentence, one that indicates what Freud thought he could publish in Austria at the time without endangering psychoanalysis: "To deprive a people of the man they take pride in as the greatest of their own is not a thing to be gladly or carelessly undertaken, least of all by someone who is himself one of them."[13] Translated into the language of Blumenberg's essay, this would mean that Freud himself was clear from the outset that he was "taking Moses the man from his people." This blow to Jewish self-confidence can thus be dated to 1937.

---

11. Freud to Zweig, 6 November 1934 and 14 March 1935, in *Letters of Sigmund Freud and Arnold Zweig*, 97, 104. Blumenberg appears to have considered Freud's doubts about the stringency of his thesis a pretext; see index cards 22761–22762, reprinted above (p. 40).

12. Freud to Anonymous, 14 December 1937, in *Letters of Sigmund Freud*, 439; cf. *SE*, 23:103–104.

13. *SE*, 23:7. At the end of the second part of *Moses and Monotheism*, Freud tried to moderate his thesis concerning the Egyptian descent of Moses by paying tribute to the prophets' part in the reconstitution of the Mosaic teachings: "It is honour enough to the Jewish people that they could preserve such a tradition and produce men who gave it a voice—even though the initiative to do it came from outside, from a great foreigner." Ibid., 51.

Yet of what is the "underestimation of the consolation denied" in publishing the complete edition of *Moses and Monotheism* in 1939 supposed to have consisted, the lack of consideration for the humiliated and persecuted Jews, of which Blumenberg accuses the exiled Freud? Freud was indeed prepared for objections on the part of the Jews. Already when sending—still from Vienna—his son Ernst a copy of the study just published in *Imago*, he mentioned a number of expectations and worries concerning it, adding: "Jewry will be very offended."[14] The most important piece of evidence in support of Blumenberg's interpretation, however, is provided by a letter from the United States that reached Freud shortly after his arrival in London at the end of June 1938 and of which he in turn told Arnold Zweig: "Just half an hour ago the post brought me a letter from a young American Jew imploring me not to deprive our poor unhappy people of the one consolation remaining to them in their misery."[15] Freud had meanwhile resumed work on the final section of the book and would no longer be deterred—neither by this letter nor by any other objections.[16]

Further clues about the history of *Moses and Monotheism* can be found in the two notes with which Freud prefaced the third part in the book edition of 1939. The dates are telling, the first being headed "[Vienna], before March, 1938," that is, before the *Anschluss* of Austria to Nazi Germany, the second "[London], June, 1938,"[17] the same month that Freud was forced to leave Vienna and found refuge in London. This suggests that Freud had already begun reworking the drafted but hitherto withheld final section in Vienna, without casting aside the reservations that had

---

14. Freud to Ernst Freud, 17 January 1938, in *Letters of Sigmund Freud*, 440. He put the matter similarly in a later letter, written on 31 October 1938 from London to Charles Singer, stating that as far as the book was concerned, which was then at the printers, "it is only Jewry and not Christianity which has reason to feel offended by its conclusions" (*Letters of Sigmund Freud*, 453).

15. Freud to Zweig, 28 June 1938, in *Letters of Sigmund Freud and Arnold Zweig*, 163.

16. Cf. also Jones, *Life and Work*, 3:207–208.

17. The square brackets were added by the editors of Freud's *Standard Edition*. (Trans.)

kept him from publication in that Catholic country. His concern for the existence of psychoanalysis endured, but was now motivated by a more general caution due to political circumstances: in early 1938, just before the German invasion, Freud did not see—or no longer saw—his opponent in the institution of the Catholic Church, hoping instead that it would prevent the rise of Nazi barbarism; indeed he felt himself "under the protection of the Catholic Church"[18] and was fearful of losing that protection. Only once this illusion had been dispelled and he, as a Jew, had to leave Austria, had he dared, he admitted in the second prefatory note, written in London, to make public the last part of his work. In free England, "there are no external obstacles remaining, or at least none to be frightened of."[19]

## III

Freud's motives for withholding parts of *Moses and Monotheism* for several years as well as for publishing the complete manuscript are thus more complicated than Blumenberg presents them. Furthermore, the fact that Freud did not release the complete text until 1939, from London, does not justify the accusation of having deprived the Jews at "the absolutely wrong moment" of "the man who, in the beginning, had founded their trust in history" (p. 1), unless one were to take the third and last part for the entire book. It certainly contained the most important sections, particularly Freud's previously withheld "investigation based on analytical assumptions of the origin of religion, specifically Jewish monotheism."[20] But Freud had already published his thesis that Moses had been an Egyptian in Vienna in 1937, and the assumption

---

18. *SE*, 23:57.
19. *SE*, 23:60.
20. Freud to Charles Singer, 31 October 1938, in *Letters of Sigmund Freud*, 453. Cf. also *SE*, 23:103: "The remainder, which included what was really open to objection and dangerous—the application [of these findings] to the genesis of monotheism and the view of religion in general—I held back, as I thought, for ever."

that the Egyptian Moses had been killed by the Jews, which Freud had adopted from archaeological studies, could already be found in the last installment published in *Imago*. It was, however, in the last section, completed in England, that he presented the fundamental hypothesis shared early on with Arnold Zweig, according to which the Jewish people owed to Moses their peculiar character, preserved across millennia, and their matchless resilience, both of which had earned them the loathing of the gentiles.[21]

Did Freud behave thoughtlessly in London? Was he "the stoic in the face of the end of the world" (p. 2), interested only in spreading his own truth and putting at stake "the self-confidence of his people" (p. 3) while Hitler was chasing the Jews out of the country and leading Europe to catastrophe? Was securing a "worthy exit" (pp. 2, 4) for himself really all he cared about? A sentence in *Moses and Monotheism* shows how important the publication of this late work was to the dying, eighty-two-year-old Freud: "I had scarcely arrived in England before I found the temptation irresistible to make the knowledge I had held back accessible to the world [. . .]."[22] But the phrase "worthy exit" is perhaps less offensive than Blumenberg thinks. It is drawn from a letter Freud wrote to his student Hanns Sachs in March 1939, in which Freud announces the publication of the book's German edition in Amsterdam and which Sachs later quoted in his memoirs—however, Freud's biographer Ernest Jones recorded another version, which sounds more modest ("The Moses is not an unworthy leavetaking").[23]

---

21. *SE*, 23:107: "[. . .] that it was the man Moses who imprinted this trait—significant for all time—upon the Jewish people. He raised their self-esteem by assuring them that they were God's chosen people, he enjoined them to holiness and pledged them to be part from others. [. . .] It was this one man Moses who created the Jews. It is to him that this people owes its tenacity of life but also much of the hostility it has experienced and still experiences."

22. *SE*, 23:103.

23. Jones, *Life and Work*, 3:259. Koestler had asked Freud to contribute an article to the weekly *Die Zukunft*, published in Paris by Willi Münzenberg. The article appeared on 25 November 1938 under the title "A Word on Anti-Semitism" ("Ein Wort zum Antisemitismus") and is collected in Sigmund Freud, *Gesammelte Werke*, Nachtragsband (Frankfurt: Fischer, 1987), 779–781. No English translation is known. See also Jones, *Life and Work*, 3:239.

There is another source for Freud's utterances in his last year, which Blumenberg surprisingly does *not* use here, though he made an excerpt from it in the same context and added it to the material for "Moses the Egyptian." During his renewed studies of Freud in the early 1980s, he became aware of Arthur Koestler's autobiography, in which Koestler recounts a visit to Freud in London in the autumn of 1938. On this occasion, Freud is reported to have said—with regard to his writings on cultural theory and group psychology—that he was not sure he could "blame" the Nazis "from his standpoint": "Well, you know, they are *abreacting* the aggression pent up in our civilisation. Something like this was inevitable, sooner or later." Koestler interpreted this as an expression of "the ethical neutrality inherent in the Freudian system—and in all strictly deterministic science."[24] To Blumenberg, who was always a collector of "last words," Freud's remark was a "last word on Nazi barbarism," spoken by one who not only, like the stoic, "fearlessly [. . .] let the world collapse over him," but who was also able "to deliver a commentary on the necessity" of its doing so. In other words: who thought himself possessed of a theory "capable of explaining what has happened and what is happening, but which in doing so prohibits any moral judgment" (p. 39). Freud was not blind to the danger National Socialism posed. But it is the theoretically founded indifference to political events in Germany that Blumenberg—who at the time, as we know, was himself in need of consolation[25]—will not forgive the old man in exile. The charge that all Freud thought about when publishing *Moses and Monotheism* in 1939 had been a "worthy exit" may thus be due not least to the memories of a then nineteen-year-old contemporary.

---

24. Koestler, *Invisible Writing*, 499.
25. Hans Blumenberg, *Der Mann vom Mond: Über Ernst Jünger*, ed. Alexander Schmitz and Marcel Lepper (Frankfurt: Suhrkamp, 2007), 87; cf. 40. See also Martin Thoemmes, "Die verzögerte Antwort: Neues über den Philosophen Hans Blumenberg," *Frankfurter Allgemeine Zeitung*, 26 March 1997; Thoemmes recounts a humiliation Blumenberg suffered in the spring of 1939 when he, though at the top of his class, was prohibited from delivering the valedictorian's speech at Lübeck's Katharineum school on account of his mother's Jewish origins; this "disgrace" is said to have been a formative experience.

## IV

How did it occur to Blumenberg that there might be "deep-rooted similarities between *Moses and Monotheism* and *Eichmann in Jerusalem*" (p. 5)? In accusing Hannah Arendt of having deprived the State of Israel of its negative founder figure, is he not merely transferring an interpretation associated with the origins of one book (Freud deprived the persecuted Jews of the founder of their religion, Moses) onto another, written under completely different historical circumstances? An undated typescript entitled "Moses the Egyptian," an early draft of the later essay, does not yet hint at any link between Freud and Arendt. The text ends abruptly, and we are never told why Blumenberg finds it "dismaying what Freud did in 1939 with 'Moses and Monotheism'" (p. 30). The first connection is made on an index card from 1976, containing notes on Arendt's book and the famous TV interview with Günter Gaus, broadcast in 1964.[26] Blumenberg states that Arendt had failed to understand a process in which there had been a "mythical necessity of archaic violence" (p. 46). And is at this point that Freud is introduced, not in order to accuse both of lack of consideration (that was added later), but to underscore Arendt's incomprehension: "Sigmund Freud should have written the book, he would have understood the dimension" (p. 46).

How could Freud provide an aid to understanding the 1961 trial, which resulted in Eichmann being condemned to death for his part in the genocide? In the later version, the above idea is restated thus: "What Freud, if he can be imagined witnessing it, would have immediately recognized is the mythical dimension of killing the negative hero of the state" (p. 11).

Had Freud, according to Blumenberg's interpretation, not himself destroyed a myth by depriving the Jews of the founder of their religion?[27] The Egyptian Moses, however, is put to death by the Jews. Hence it is the Freudian story of the murder of the primal

---

26. See above, p. 45, n. 9.
27. That myth was not "brought to an end" in *Moses and Monotheism* is an idea Blumenberg expressed elegantly with reference to Freud's meeting with Thomas Mann in Vienna (see above, p. 34). At the time, one was working on the

horde's father by his sons, developed in *Totem and Taboo* and reiterated in *Moses and Monotheism*, whose mythic potential Blumenberg summons as a corrective to Arendt's account of the Eichmann trial. Yet this comes at a price, for it leads to an interpretation of that trial and the historical events examined therein that is quite problematic indeed. Blumenberg challenges us to consider the following comparison: Moses, the liberator and legislator of the Jews and founder of their religion, was killed, but he created the conditions of possibility of the survival of the Jewish people. Eichmann, the organizer of the murder of the Jews and negative founder of their state, "must be killed, like Moses, although he created the conditions of possibility of this nationhood" (p. 5). But were Moses and Eichmann really "founder figures" in equal measure, one positive and the other negative? What does the resilience that Moses imparted to the Jews in the course of a "forty-year education in the desert" (p. 1) have to do with the foundation of a Jewish state as a response to Hitler's destructive mania? Can the murder of Moses, transferred to the realm of the archaic, be connected with the death sentence on Eichmann? It remains to be shown what the consequences are when Blumenberg speaks of a "mythical dimension" of the Jerusalem trial that had to be understood.

# V

It seems that Hannah Arendt and Hans Blumenberg met only once, briefly, in November 1956. No correspondence is preserved, and their respective writings bear little trace of an engagement with the other's work.[28] No evidence has yet come to light of a noisy

---

greatest of his epic works, the tetralogy *Joseph and His Brothers*, while the other was putting to paper his speculations concerning Moses's Egyptian descent: "Both were contributing, in their own ways, to the myth of a mythless god, who tolerated no images or stories around him." Blumenberg, *Work on Myth*, 516.

28. Blumenberg, *Legitimacy of the Modern Age*, 8–9; Hannah Arendt, *The Life of the Mind*, 2 vols. in 1 (New York: Harcourt Brace, 1981), 113, 226n24, 233n39. Arendt's (inexact) quotations suggest that Blumenberg was sending her offprints as late as the early 1970s. See also Blumenberg, *Quellen, Ströme, Eisberge*, 250.

personal falling out between the two. Yet Blumenberg's criticisms of this student of Heidegger's, who fled Germany in 1933, could barely be harsher and seems comparable only to the verdict of Gershom Scholem, who, on publication of the American edition of *Eichmann in Jerusalem* in 1963, accused Arendt of lacking in "love of the Jewish people." But the argument with Arendt, which makes up the second part of the Moses essay, is of a later date. What may have prompted Blumenberg to return to the Eichmann book at a time when the public controversy surrounding it had long ebbed?

There is some evidence that it was his long-standing interest in questions of mythology in the preliminary stages of *Work on Myth* (the book was published in 1979) that first turned Blumenberg's attention to the problematic aspects of Arendt's account. As mentioned above, his first charge, in his 1976 notes on the interview with Günter Gaus, was that the political scientist had failed to grasp the "mythical necessity" of Eichmann's sentencing and execution. Aside from one published review, Blumenberg's Nachlass contains scant evidence of an early reception of Arendt's theory of totalitarianism. In 1946, immediately upon the publication of the German version of Arendt's essay "Organized Guilt" in the journal *Die Wandlung*,[29] he excerpted—clearly with a particular motive in mind—a longer passage dealing with the role of family men in Himmler's organization. This emphasis also marks the review—not altogether devoid of errors—that Blumenberg devoted to Arendt's *Sechs Essays*, published in 1948.[30] On the other hand, as far as can be told, he paid no close attention, neither at the time nor later, to Arendt's magnum opus, *The Origins of Totalitarianism*, a German translation of which was published in 1955.

Blumenberg's own reading logs suggest that he did not work his way through *Eichmann in Jerusalem* completely until 1978, more than two years after Arendt's death, making extensive notes on

---

29. See above, pp. 41–43.
30. See above, pp. 43–45. What is striking is Blumenberg's misinterpretation of the term "pariah," which Arendt uses to describe the experience of Jews as outsiders, and which Blumenberg confuses with the "mob" or underclass created by imperialism.

index cards in the process.[31] Taken as sketches, they are in some respects clearer and more revealing, their judgments more nuanced, than the fully developed text into which they were absorbed and which Blumenberg—now incorporating the aforementioned material on Freud's late work, collected from 1975 to 1982—committed to paper a decade later under the title "Moses the Egyptian," only to put it aside, like so much else, as incomplete. Further support for this dating can be found in the phrase "viewed another quarter century later" (p. 7), with which Blumenberg describes the time elapsed between the publication of Arendt's book in 1963 and his own critical reappraisal. Taken together, the long interval and the sharpness of his argumentation suggest that this particular "viewer" found the subject, for reasons connected with his own biography, to be very close to home indeed.

## VI

One of the greatest surprises of the text presented here is that Blumenberg's polemic against Arendt follows a decidedly Zionist narrative. Unlike the courtroom critic of "the play aspect of trial," which she did not even attend in its entirety, Blumenberg sides with the historical-political intentions of the then Israeli government and with the prosecution, which followed political instructions. Both wanted to make of the trial a didactic play against anti-Semitism. He rejects the suggestion made not only by Arendt, but also by Karl Jaspers and others, to have Eichmann tried by an international tribunal and the murder of the Jews punished as a "crime against humanity." To do so would have removed the Holocaust from Jewish history. Instead, he defends the right of the State of Israel and its people of survivors to

---

31. The journal *Merkur* (vol. 17, no. 186, pp. 759–776) published an excerpt from Arendt's report, which Blumenberg read at the time, but on which there are no remarks in his notes. He is likely to have followed reports of the so-called Arendt controversy in the media, but all the information used in the essay presented here derived exclusively from the version published as a book.

try their professed enemy before an Israeli court for "crimes against the Jewish people." The fundamental difference between Arendt and Blumenberg is expressed in the following sentence: "As a crime against humanity, [. . .] the case of Eichmann would have been 'internationalized,' not a crime of the most monstrous singularity against the Jewish people and not the warrant, impervious to any realistic objection, for [the foundation of] this state" (p. 10). Blumenberg thus fundamentally rejects any universalistic reading of the Holocaust of the kind found—albeit refracted through an explicitly "Jewish" lens—not least in the work of Hannah Arendt.[32]

To refer to Eichmann as the negative founder of the State of Israel is to adopt a decided position toward Judaism and its catastrophe in the twentieth century that one would barely have expected from Hans Blumenberg. But does this position not have at its heart a philosophy of history that bestows meaning on this catastrophe after the fact?[33] In one of the essay's dark passages, Blumenberg, with regard to Freud's Egyptian Moses, speaks of the "mechanism of repetition, in which a stranger, one possessed by the frenzy of blood, would once more renew the sublimating chastisements of the desert and yet, in the wildest autism, serve only the historical interest of the chastised" (p. 3). This stranger was Hitler. And in the way that Moses, who sought to subject the Jewish people to an alien god, could from the perspective of history become a tool of that people by teaching them an "art of survival" that enabled them to withstand all future catastrophes ("all future deserts and captivities" [p. 4]), so Hitler, too—if one wishes to follow Blumenberg's text—pursued the "historical interest" of the Jews.[34]

---

32. Cf. Dan Diner, "Hannah Arendt Reconsidered: On the Banal and the Evil in Her Holocaust Narrative," *New German Critique* 71 (Spring–Summer 1997): 177–190, esp. 179.

33. An unpublished text is not safe from readings that the author can never have intended. Yet one cannot but wonder what meaning Blumenberg may have had in mind when he wrote that it had been Eichmann's function to enter "the national myth as the vanquished necessary enemy, who may have claimed victims but, in doing so, had foisted upon their sacrifice the only meaning still possible" (p. 9).

34. It is no coincidence that the passage ends with a mention of Augustine's *felix culpa* argument; see above, p. 4.

The founding of a Jewish state after the Holocaust would prove this point.

It must have escaped Blumenberg that Eichmann's defense counsel, Robert Servatius, unfortunately pursued a similar argument in order to demonstrate the absurdity of the charges. As Harry Mulisch and Robert Pendorf, two other observers of the trial, reported more accurately than Arendt, Servatius, unafraid of embarrassing himself, began to extemporize to the court on the "spirit in history, which moves forward by necessity and without human intervention," and which often turned the will and actions of individuals upside down. In the case at hand, Hitler had tried to exterminate the Jews, but instead a thriving Jewish state had come into being. According to this theory, Mulisch wrote, Eichmann appeared as "the actual founder of the State of Israel."[35]

Servatius struck at the heart of Zionist self-understanding. From an opposed angle, Arendt accused the Israeli leadership of instrumentalizing the Eichmann trial and the story of Jewish suffering to prove to the world the necessity of the founding of a Jewish state. Underlying this stance was her fundamental objection to Zionism as an ideology of legitimation. This is another point on which she and Blumenberg disagree: in her little-known answer to questions put by the American journalist Samuel Grafton in 1963, Arendt, alluding to the temporary cooperation between Zionists and Nazis on matters of emigration to Palestine and hinting at the problem of evil, wrote: "But the trouble is that European Zionism [. . .] has often thought and said that the evil of antisemitism [sic] was necessary for the good of the Jewish people. In the words of a well-known Zionist in a letter to me discussing 'the original Zionist argumentation: The antisemites want to get rid of the Jews, the Jewish State wants to receive them, a

---

35. Harry Mulisch, *Criminal Case 40/61, the Trial of Adolf Eichmann: An Eyewitness Account* (1961), trans. Robert Naborn (Philadelphia: University of Pennsylvania Press, 2005), 64. Cf. also Robert Pendorf, "Der Verteidiger Eichmanns," *Die Zeit*, 5 May 1961; and *EJ*, 19–20. What is harder still to stomach is that Eichmann himself had put similar ideas on record even in his exile in Argentina: "Every German act of violence against Jewry [was] a building block of the Israelite [sic] state" (quoted in Wojak, *Eichmanns Memoiren*, 58).

perfect match.' The notion that we can use our enemies for our own salvation has always been to me the 'original sin' of Zionism."[36]

It also seems problematic that Blumenberg should use the tainted term "state of exception" to describe the dimensions of the Jerusalem trial, to which "no law [. . .] but that of unique historic right" (p. 10) had applied—whereas Arendt saw "everything juridically." Arendt would barely have denied that there was no precedent for Eichmann's trial and execution because the crime he was sentenced for was unprecedented, although she considered the application of Israel's Nazis and Nazi Collaborators (Punishment) Law, which the Knesset had passed in 1950, inappropriate in the light of the facts of the case as they were presented. And that the Germans too should have wished to put Hitler on trial or to have had their own "Nuremberg," this imperative of Blumenberg's would also not have been controversial between them.

But the great philosopher, who began as a proponent of the Enlightenment, later on appears to have been convinced "that we still need myths," as Karl Heinz Bohrer put it following the publication of Blumenberg's *Work on Myth*,[37] even "new myths," which Blumenberg had once cautioned against.[38] Blumenberg remythicizes the Eichmann trial, that is to say, he translates it into a mythological

---

36. Arendt, *Jewish Writings*, 479. In her response, Arendt also mentioned Servatius's performance; see below, p. 92, n. 53.
37. Karl Heinz Bohrer, "Rückkehr des Mythos?," *Frankfurter Allgemeine Zeitung*, 26 January 1980.
38. Cf. Hans Blumenberg, Jacob Taubes, *Briefwechsel 1961–1981*, ed. Herbert Kopp-Oberstebrink and Martin Treml (Berlin: Suhrkamp, 2013), 256 (note dated 1968). "New myths" were discussed at the Fourth Congress of the research group Poetik und Hermeneutik in 1968, however—following a distinction made by the Slavist Jurij Striedter—"old myths in new functions" rather more than "'new myths' in old functions" (Fuhrmann, *Terror und Spiel*, 679). In 1974, Blumenberg recorded the following under the heading "Remythicization": "Motivations; The subject of myth belongs to the pathology of reason" (Index card 15801, card file 16). See also Blumenberg, *Work on Myth*, 29, 35, 99–100, and passim. *Präfiguration*, a text recently released from the Nachlass, shows that Blumenberg—in the tradition of Ernst Cassirer—did indeed engage critically with the continued virulence of mythical patterns of thought in the shape of modern political myths; Hans Blumenberg, *Präfiguration: Arbeit am politischen Mythos*, ed. Angus Nicholls and Felix Heidenreich (Berlin: Suhrkamp, 2014).

scenario that places the punishment of the Nazi murder of the Jews in an archaic context of revenge and the slaughter of enemies. This is the purpose of referring back to *Moses and Monotheism*. Arendt, incidentally, is by no means as much a stranger to such "long-forgotten propositions" (p. 10) as Blumenberg supposes. He mistakenly reads her agreement with similar reflections by the American constitutional lawyer Yosal Rogat, with which she introduces her own summing-up against Eichmann, as their rejection.[39] It is telling that in doing so, he should happen to misread the very passages in her book in which their positions are closest.

What is more, myth offers—this, besides that of consolation, is one of the functions Blumenberg ascribes to it—intuitiveness[40] where the limits of analysis are reached. This is why it was not permissible, in Jerusalem, to speak of German society, which had brought forth the murderous bureaucrats, and not of the share of the guilt of others, who hid behind the defendant. Not that Blumenberg failed to see the scandal of the nonpunishment of Nazi criminals in the Federal Republic, to which Arendt wished to draw attention. "I do not disapprove of this tendency [in *Eichmann in Jerusalem*]," Blumenberg could still note in the late 1970s (p. 52), but it came at the expense of Eichmann's singular significance for the Jewish state. The "mythical act," as Blumenberg understands the trial, needed a figure to concentrate on. Eichmann had to be the sole culprit, a surface for the projections not least of the witnesses to the trial and the surviving victims, a scapegoat that embodied all the misdeeds visited upon the Jews.

## VII

On the other hand, Blumenberg indeed succeeds in identifying the weaknesses of *Eichmann in Jerusalem*. These include the disregard for most of the prosecution witnesses, largely survivors of

---

39. *EJ*, 277; Rogat, *Eichmann Trial and the Rule of Law*; see above, p. 25, n. 87.
40. *Veranschaulichung*; see above, p. 22, n. 72. (Trans.)

the ghettos and death camps, whom the intellectual flown in from New York reproaches for accusing Eichmann of crimes he could not have committed. Today, it is precisely in the appearance of contemporary witnesses and the beginning of talking about Auschwitz that we see the significance of the Jerusalem trial. Arendt's blanket charge of collaboration leveled against the *Judenräte* and other compulsory organizations installed by the Nazis was already refuted by most critics in the course of the controversy over her book in the 1960s. Historians have since reached a more complex understanding of events. Blumenberg adds an argument that is of the greatest significance for understanding the Holocaust: who among the persecuted and among those who were forced to negotiate with the Nazis could know that a genocide was to be at the end of it all? With the exception of the regions in which the killing took place, knowledge of the mass murder of Jews in German-occupied Europe spread only late and very hesitantly. "But it was a reality of the incredible, which nobody can be expected to reckon with. What Hannah Arendt demands is to have thought the incredible" (p. 6).[41]

Arendt's most unbearable sentence, made worse in the German edition by being supported with information provided by the Dutch historian Louis de Jong,[42] reads: "The whole truth was that if the Jewish people had really been unorganized and leaderless, there would have been chaos and plenty of misery but the total number of victims would hardly have been between four and a half and six million."[43] Blumenberg asks whether Arendt had really believed that. She did believe it, for she presented, with reference to de Jong, a cruel calculation, according to which half of those deported could have saved themselves from destruction had they not followed the instructions of the Jewish Council. Her reckoning

---

41. See above, p. 18, n. 45.
42. Louis de Jong to Hannah Arendt, 21 August 1963, Hannah Arendt Papers, Correspondence, copy from the Library of Congress at the Hannah-Arendt-Zentrum at the University of Oldenburg; not online. Arendt misinterpreted de Jong's figures; see above, p. 18, n. 44.
43. *EJ*, 125; *EJG*, 162.

with Zionism and its representatives thus culminates in the merciless accusation of the "compliance of the victims."[44]

Another contentious issue in the controversy was the book's subtitle. Looking back, one must say that Arendt did not do enough to insure her dictum "the banality of evil" against misunderstanding. She clearly wanted something to oppose to the "demonization" of Eichmann by the prosecution, and she insisted, as though this were the most natural thing, that the accused be brought to justice personally for his own deeds, and only for them. Yet her few comments, scattered throughout the text, concerning Eichmann as the incarnation of a new, hitherto unknown type of criminal, that of the "administrative murderer" [*Verwaltungsmörder*] and his "inability to *think*" were not sufficient to justify the supposed banality of evil.[45] Nor did her claim that Eichmann's "was obviously also no case of insane hatred of Jews, of fanatical anti-Semitism or indoctrination of any kind"[46] help to clear up the facts of the matter, and was bound to be challenged.

---

44. *Die Fügsamkeit der Opfer* (*EJG*, 151). The corresponding passage in the English version: "Mere compliance would never have been enough [. . .]" (*EJ*, 115). (Trans.)

45. *EJG*, 15–16, 324; *EJ*, 49, 273–276. Arendt explained her book's subtitle more convincingly in a 1964 radio interview with Joachim Fest: "Let me tell you what I mean by banality, since in Jerusalem I remembered a story that Ernst Jünger once recounted and that I'd forgotten." Arendt had read this story, which she recounted from memory, during her first postwar visit to Germany in 1949/50, in Ernst Jünger's diaries: "Kirchhorst, 12 May 1942. Drove to the barber's. Discussed the Russian prisoners, who are being sent to work from the camps. 'There are supposed to be some bad eggs among them. They'll steal the dogs' food.' Recorded verbatim. One often has the impression that the German burgher is ridden by the Devil." Ernst Jünger, *Strahlungen* (Tübingen: Heliopolis, 1949), 117. Arendt added the following commentary to the story: "You see, there's something outrageously stupid about this story. [. . .] Eichmann was perfectly intelligent, but in this respect he was stupid. It was this stupidity that was outrageous. And that was what I actually meant by banality. There's nothing deep about it—nothing demonic! There's simply the reluctance ever to imagine what the other person is experiencing, right?" ("Eichmann Was Outrageously Stupid," 47–48). Cf. Hannah Arendt, "The Aftermath of Nazi Rule—Report from Germany," *Commentary* 10 (1950): 342–352, 348. See also below, p. 50, n. 53.

46. *EJ*, 26.

In the prologue to the German edition, Arendt explained that she had explained nothing but a "phenomenon" that "it was impossible to ignore."[47] The accused had "deprived himself of any demonic aura."[48] The picture she drew of Eichmann seems then initially to have referred only to the obvious discrepancy between the insignificant man in the glass box and the monstrosity of the crimes of which he was accused.[49] Only from Arendt's correspondence as well as her later lectures and posthumously collected notes can the outlines of a theory of evil that dispenses with any theological or metaphysical justification be retraced.[50] In *The Origins of Totalitarianism*, she had still used the Kantian idea of "radical evil."[51] "I changed my mind," she wrote to Scholem

---

47. *EJG*, 15.
48. "Eichmann Was Outrageously Stupid," 46.
49. "I was struck by a manifest shallowness in the doer that made it impossible to trace the uncontestable evil of his deeds to any deeper level of roots or motives. The deeds were monstrous, but the doer—at least the very effective one now on trial—was quite ordinary, commonplace, and neither demonic nor monstrous." Arendt, *Life of the Mind*, 4. In relation to this, the question, again much discussed of late, of whether Eichmann might not have been the bureaucrat and subaltern functionary that he pretended to be in Jerusalem and whether Arendt might even have been "duped" by him, seems of little consequence. Cf. Bettina Stangneth, *Eichmann before Jerusalem: The Unexamined Life of a Mass Murderer* (2011) (New York: Knopf, 2014); and the interview with the author in *Die Welt*, published online, 4 April 2011, http://www.welt.de/13063495: "I was sure that [Eichmann] had lied to a previously unsuspected extent in Jerusalem. But I had to prove it. That he pulled off a shameless show, by which Hannah Arendt too was duped."
50. Cf. Arendt, *Life of the Mind*, 3–4; Arendt, "Some Questions of Moral Philosophy" (1965–66), in *Responsibility and Judgment*, 49–146, 95, 111–112, 146; Arendt, *Denktagebuch*, ed. Ursula Ludz and Ingeborg Nordmann (Munich: Piper, 2002), 622–623. Arendt based her ideas about the connection between thought and morality on Kant's concept of the "enlarged mentality" (*erweiterte Denkungsart*; Kant, *Critique of Judgment*, §40); see Arendt, "The Crisis in Culture," in *Between Past and Future*, ed. Jerome Kohn (New York: Penguin, 2006), 194–222, esp. 217; and Arendt, *Denktagebuch*, 570, 603.
51. Hannah Arendt, *The Origins of Totalitarianism* (1951) 3rd ed. (San Diego, New York, and London: Harcourt, 1973), ix, 443, 459; the concept of "radical evil" can be found in Immanuel Kant, *Religion within the Boundaries of Mere Reason and Other Writings*, ed. Allen Wood and George Di Giovanni (Cambridge: Cambridge University Press, 1999), 45.

in 1963,[52] and in the reply to Grafton cited above she described the evil of which Eichmann was the prototype as "a surface phenomenon," possessing "no depth" and with nothing "demonic" about it: "Instead of being radical, it is merely extreme."[53] Arendt overlooked that this definition might contradict the experiences of the persecuted.

Surprisingly, it is not so much Arendt's phrase "the banality of evil" that really upset Blumenberg as her description of Eichmann as a "clown" (a word that, it should be noted, she had adopted from the records of Eichmann's interrogation).[54] Blumenberg sees it as the continuation of her earlier concept of totalitarianism, according to which "family men" and "petit bourgeois run wild" had become compliant murderers under National Socialism. As already discussed, however, it seems rather doubtful that Blumenberg knew Arendt's book *The Origins of Totalitarianism*, for he refers here to the early essay "Organized Guilt and Universal Responsibility." In this first analysis of the Nazi regime's mass support,

---

52. Arendt/Scholem, *Briefwechsel*, 444; see also Jaspers to Arendt, 22 October 1963: "Now you have delivered the crucial blow against 'radical evil,' against gnosis!" (Arendt/Jaspers, *Correspondence*, 525).

53. Arendt, *Jewish Writings*, 479: "Moreover, as the phrase now stands—'banality of evil'—it is contrasted with 'radical evil' (Kant) and, more popularly, with the widely held opinion that there is something demonic, grandiose, in great evil, that there is even such a thing as the power of evil to bring forth something good. Mephisto in *Faust* is the *Geist der stets das Böse will und stets das Gute schafft*; the devil seen as a fallen angel (Lucifer) suggests that the best are most likely to become the worst; Hegel's whole philosophy rests on the 'power of negation,' of necessity, for instance, to bring about 'the realm of freedom,' and so on. The question came up in the trial through Servatius on the most vulgar level of course. [. . .] I meant that evil is not radical, going to the roots (*radix*), that it has no depth, and that for this very reason it is so terribly difficult to think about, since thinking, by definition, wants to reach the roots. Evil is a surface phenomenon, and instead of being radical, it is merely extreme." Arendt's use of metaphors of "depth" and "surface," "rootedness," "uprooting," and "shallowness," in this context can likely be traced to Heidegger. Blumenberg himself at one point spoke of a "drastic 'superficiality'" about the syndrome of anti-Semitism and rejected demonizing explanations for the Holocaust (see above, pp. 62–63); in doing so, he came closer to Arendt's explanations than he would have cared to admit.

54. See above, p. 24, n. 78.

Arendt describes Himmler and his murderous troops as "'bourgeois' with [. . .] all the habits of a good *paterfamilias*," whose conscience was relieved by the functional character of their actions. This might also be said of Eichmann, but does not get to the heart of the examination of evil under conditions of totalitarianism, which was Arendt's later project. In his indignation at seeing ridiculed the man he wanted to be understood as the "negative national hero" of Israel, Blumenberg prevents himself from understanding what Arendt meant when she spoke of the "banality of evil." And he fails to do justice to her ceaseless efforts to find concepts able to make sense of the unprecedented horrors of Auschwitz.

## VIII

Blumenberg was known for assiduously avoiding serious discussion of some contemporary thinkers—for instance, Theodor W. Adorno or Jürgen Habermas—and resorting to blanket judgments that, at best, displayed some sense of irony. Nobody will say this about his response to Arendt's *Eichmann in Jerusalem*, the postponed reading of which must have hurt him quite considerably. In his own lifetime, Blumenberg hardly ever discussed his own situation under the Nazi regime, less still his own family background, which had made him a *Halbjude* according to Nazi racial doctrine.[55] His posthumous papers and the essay "Moses the Egyptian" published here show that an interest in Judaism was a hidden constant in his life.

---

55. His texts, too, contain only a few hints; e.g., in Blumenberg, *Ein mögliches Selbstverständnis*, 22–23, 81–82; Blumenberg, *Die Verführbarkeit des Philosophen*, edited in association with Manfred Sommer by the Hans Blumenberg-Archiv (Frankfurt: Suhrkamp 2000), 76; see also p. 80, n. 25 above.

# Editorial Note and Acknowledgments

The typescript of the essay "Moses the Egyptian" ("Moses der Ägypter") can be found in the papers of Hans Blumenberg, kept at the Deutsches Literaturarchiv Marbach. The original, which was clearly typed to dictation and contains a few amendments in Blumenberg's hand, runs to eleven pages and is part of a collection entitled "Text- und Materialsammlung Moses der Ägypter," which also contains other drafts published here. The pages are numbered UNF 350–360; the use of two different typewriter fonts suggests repeated revisions. Blumenberg, probably ironically, referred to the short texts under the heading UNF as "unerlaubte Fragmente" (forbidden fragments), though the actual meaning was more likely *unfertig*, "incomplete," designating drafts to be drawn upon later. Although UNF 1 to 400 were dictated between 1973 and 1981, there is reason to suppose that UNF 350–360 was composed later, as the text itself suggests: "a quarter century" after the publication of Hannah Arendt's book *Eichmann in Jerusalem*. Most of the other texts from the Marbach Nachlass first published in the present volume—particularly excerpts and notes made on index cards—can be dated with some precision, for Blumenberg maintained detailed records of the cards added to his files year for year. According to these records, the material on Freud was compiled between 1975 and 1982, that on Arendt largely in 1978.

The present edition spells out Blumenberg's abbreviations and incorporates his corrections; underlinings are shown in italics, including those added for emphasis within excerpts. Errors of transcription of mishearings in dictation have been pointed out only where they result in a change of meaning.

It was Rüdiger Zill of Potsdam who first recognized the significance of the Moses fragment and presented it at a conference in February 2009.[56] Part of the essay was published in the *Neue Zürcher Zeitung* on 1 March 2014 under the title "Eichmann—der 'negative' Held des Staates Israel."[57]

---

56. See *Frankfurter Allgemeine Zeitung*, 11 February 2009.
57. Published online at http://www.nzz.ch/eichmann—der-negative-held-des-staates-israel-1.18253335.

I am grateful to the Deutsches Literaturarchiv Marbach and to Bettina Blumenberg for their kind permission to publish the texts collected here. Bettina Blumenberg supported the publication from the outset. Her advice was as helpful as her critical questions were. My thanks go not least to Dorit Krusche, who catalogued Blumenberg's Nachlass at the Marbach archive. Without her support, this volume could not have appeared in its present form.

## Translator's Note

Regarding the presentation of the text, I have standardized the italicization of book titles and the use of quotation marks only in the central text, "Moses the Egyptian." Elsewhere, Blumenberg's use of quotation marks is largely retained, as are his in-line citations. The notes throughout are by Ahlrich Meyer unless otherwise specified. My own notes or additions to existing notes are signed (Trans.) and are enclosed in [square brackets] where necessary to distinguish them from the editor's.

Wherever possible, references are to the English versions of texts originally cited in German. Abbreviations are used for the following frequently cited works.

EJ     *Eichmann in Jerusalem*
Hannah Arendt. *Eichmann in Jerusalem: A Report on the Banality of Evil*. Revised and enlarged edition, 1965. New York: Penguin, 1994. The frequently reprinted and most commonly available paperback edition.

EJG     *Eichmann in Jerusalem* (German)
Hannah Arendt. *Eichmann in Jerusalem: Ein Bericht von der Banalität des Bösen*. Translated by Brigitte Grantzow and revised and expanded by the author. Munich: Piper, 1964. The first German edition, and the one with which Blumenberg appears to have worked. Its pagination differs from the German edition available today.

SE     *Standard Edition*
Sigmund Freud. *The Standard Edition of the Complete Psychological Works of Sigmund Freud*. Translated from the German under the general editorship of James Strachey, in collaboration with Anna Freud. 24 vols. London: The Hogarth Press, 1964. The text most frequently referred to here, *Moses and Monotheism*, is found in *SE*, 23:1–137. The text of the original, separately published English edition differs from that collected in the *Standard Edition* in many phrasings. Both English versions are credited to Katherine Jones as translator.

# Translator's Note

I am grateful to Peter Uwe Hohendahl and the editorial board of *Signale* for giving me the opportunity to translate this book. Paul Fleming did much to improve this translation by being kind enough to make many helpful comments on earlier drafts. At Cornell, I wish to thank Kizer Walker and Marian Rogers for their help in preparing the manuscript. For their support and encouragement at earlier stages of this project, my thanks go Bettina Blumenberg, Petra Hardt (Suhrkamp Verlag), Dorit Krusche (DLA Marbach), and Anson Rabinbach (Princeton University).

## Illustration Credits

Figs. 1–3, pp. 67–69: Deutsches Literaturarchiv Marbach, Nachlass Hans Blumenberg

## About the Authors

Hans Blumenberg (1920–1996) was professor of philosophy emeritus at the University of Münster and the author of numerous books, including *Paradigms for a Metaphorology* (also in Cornell's Signale series), *The Legitimacy of the Modern Age*, *The Genesis of the Copernican World*, and *Work on Myth*.

Ahlrich Meyer was born in 1941 and was, until his retirement, professor of political science, specializing in political theories, at the University of Oldenburg. He is currently in charge of a project studying the persecution of Jews in Western Europe, funded by the German Research Community (Deutsche Forschungsgemeinschaft).

www.ingramcontent.com/pod-product-compliance
Lightning Source LLC
Chambersburg PA
CBHW032007150725
29645CB00023B/447